Auf geht's - sprechen Sie Deutsch!

This edition published 2003 by Caxton Editions an imprint of
The Caxton Publishing Group under Licence from Carrousel MS.
ISBN 184067 4490
Reprint 2006
©2002 by Carrousel MS. Paris
Photos: Corel Professional Photos, Photo Disc, project photos
Printed in China

Instruction

This Audio Course in German will help you to improve and refresh your present abilities in the German language. Even if you have little or no previous knowledge of German, you will find this course provides you with a quick and systematic introduction to your "new" language.

You will find 12 chapters on these CDs and in the accompanying textbook. Each chapter concentrates on a particular theme and typical situations where German is spoken.

At the beginning you will read or listen to a dialogue or a conversation that introduces you to the topic of each new lesson. Additionally, you will find exercises that relate directly to these themes. After that, you will be asked to respond to certain phrases of a conversation partner. The CD has built-in pauses to allow you to respond to each statement. These practice exercises will allow you to practice and improve your knowledge of standard spoken German expressions that occur in realistic situations.

In the next section you will find explanations for the grammar that you will need to master the language. The distribution of grammar is not only designed to help you with each relevant situation in every chapter, but also to allow you to learn the grammar in a traditional, step-by-step fashion.

It is especially important for beginners to be able to learn the necessary aspects of a language in a comfortable and logical manner. If you are an advanced language learner, you need not follow the lessons step-by-step; instead it is recommended that you select lessons with topics that interest you. Here the grammar lessons should serve primarily to reinforce your existing knowledge of German.

At the conclusion of the lesson you will find typical informations about the country. These will contain such diverse subjects as:

- Important idioms of everyday conversation that you should know;
- The social customs you will need to know;
- Information that explains typical ways of behaviour;
- Historical and cultural information.

In the last part of the chapter you will find additional exercises relating to the entire lesson contents. For these exercises you write your answers. An answer key at the back of the book allows you to check your answers.

Additionally you will find a comprehensive glossary and listings of grammar forms.

Technical instructions:
Insert the desired CD in your CD drive and press the start key. A narrator will guide you through the programme. The pauses where you will be asked to respond ver-

bally will always be announced well in advance. If you decide these pauses are too short for your taste, or if you wish to pause anywhere in the programme, simply press the pause key of your CD player. You can also go back to any desired section earlier in a lesson.

We wish you all the best with your German lessons!

Course information

This CD course will help you to not only learn important language forms in German but also to deepen your knowledge of German grammar.

The exercises to the individual lessons are not directly related to the dialogues that come earlier.

This allows you to complete each lesson without having to go back and listen again to the dialogue. With the dialogue, you can concentrate entirely on the language, without having to always worry about having to memorise all the information it contains for later questions.

These exercises are designed to test your language ability, not your memory capabilities.

If you do find that you have problems with an exercise, we recommend that you go directly to the grammar section of the lesson. There you will find the information that will help you to find the necessary answers.

Lektion/Lesson	Seite/Page

CD1
TOP1 Hello! In this Lesson I would like to give you some information that can help you to feel "at home" when you arrive in Germany. You will find dialogues with the following themes:

– How to make contact with someone for the first time,
– How to ask for information,
– How to say thanks.

At first you should listen to, read and repeat the following sentences, as you will hear these sentences frequently in conversation and can use them often.

Important phrases:
First, listen to these phrases:

Guten Morgen	Good morning
Guten Tag	Hello
Guten Abend	Good evening
Gute Nacht	Good night
Auf Wiedersehen	Goodbye
Tschüss	Bye
Herzlich willkommen	Welcome
Ich habe eine Frage.	I have a question.
Können Sie mir bitte sagen ...	Could you tell me...
Danke	Thank you
Bitte	Please
Entschuldigung	Excuse me
Tut mir Leid	I'm sorry

Now listen to the following dialogue.

Dialog / Dialogue

Andreas:
Guten Tag. Herzlich willkommen, ich möchte Sie in Deutschland begrüßen.

Andreas:
Hello. I'd like to welcome you to Germany.

Mishiko:
Guten Tag. Danke für die freundliche Begrüßung.

Mishiko:
Hello. Thanks for your hospitality.

Andreas:
Bitte, es ist mir eine Freude, Sie kennen zu lernen.

Andreas:
It's a pleasure to meet you. You're welcome.

Mishiko:
Entschuldigung, aber mein Deutsch ist nicht sehr gut.

Mishiko:
Please excuse my German. It's not very good.

Andreas:
Ich werde Ihnen helfen. Sie sprechen aber doch schon gut Deutsch.
Sind Sie das erste Mal in Deutschland?

Andreas:
I'll help you. But you already speak German well.
Is this your first time in Germany?

Mishiko:
Nein, ich war vor zwei Jahren schon einmal in Deutschland.

No, I was here once before, two years ago.

Andreas:
Wo waren Sie in Deutschland?

Andreas:
Where did you visit in Germany?

Mishiko:
Ich habe Berlin besucht.

Mishiko:
I visited Berlin.

Andreas:
Berlin ist eine schöne Stadt.

Andreas:
Berlin is a beautiful city.

Mishiko:
Ja, es hat mir dort sehr gut gefallen.
Waren Sie auch schon in Japan?

Mishiko:
Yes, I liked it very much.
Have you ever been to Japan?

Andreas:
Nein, leider war ich noch nicht dort.
Aus welcher japanischen Stadt kommen Sie?

Andreas:
No, unfortunately not.
Which Japanese city do you come from?

Mishiko:
Ich komme aus Tokio und aus welcher Stadt kommen Sie?

Mishiko:
I come from Tokyo. Which city do you come from?

Andreas:
Ich komme aus Köln.

Andreas:
I come from Cologne.

Mishiko:
Köln liegt doch am Rhein, oder?

Mishiko:
Cologne is on the Rhine river, isn't it?

Andreas:
Ja, richtig. Köln ist die größte Stadt am Rhein.

Andreas:
Yes, that's right. Cologne is the biggest city on the Rhine.

Mishiko:
Ich hoffe, dass ich den Rhein auch sehen werde. Es soll dort sehr schön sein.

Mishiko:
I hope to also visit the Rhine. I hear it's quite pretty there.

Andreas:
Es ist wunderschön dort. Wenn Sie möchten, besorge ich Karten für eine Schifffahrt auf dem Rhein.

Andreas:
It's beautiful there. If you like, I can get some tickets for a boat ride down the Rhine.

Mishiko:
Eine sehr gute Idee. Ich freue mich darauf.

Mishiko:
A very good idea. I would like that a lot.

Andreas:
Schön. Jetzt zeige ich Ihnen aber erst Ihr Hotel, in dem Sie wohnen werden.

Andreas:
Great. Now I'll show you your hotel.

I recommend that you listen to the whole dialogue a second time. You should now repeat the individual sentences, so that you can get a feeling for the correct responses.
(If the dialogue is too fast, please use the pause button on your CD player.)

CD1
TOP2

Übung 1 / Exercise 1:

- In this Exercise you will hear a few questions that you should respond to.
- First listen to the question;
- A signal tone will follow;
- Then you should say your answer;
- Then you will hear the correct answer, which will allow you to check to see if you answered correctly.

B Beispiel/Example:

Sprecher:	*Kommt Andreas aus Köln?*
Speaker:	*Does Andreas come from Cologne?*
Sie:	*Ja, er kommt aus Köln.*
You:	*Yes, he comes from Cologne.*
Sprecher:	*Kommt Mishiko aus Tokio?*
Speaker:	*Does Mishiko come from Tokyo?*
Sie:	*Ja, sie kommt aus Tokio.*
You:	*Yes, she comes from Tokyo.*

1.
2.
3.

Exercise:

1. Kommt Andreas aus Köln?
   Ja, er kommt aus Köln.

   Does Andreas come from Cologne?
   Yes, he come from Cologne.

2. Kommt Mishiko aus Tokio?
   Ja, sie kommt aus Tokio.

   Does Mishiko come from Tokio?
   Yes, she comes from Tokyo

3. Liegt Köln am Rhein?
   Ja, Köln liegt am Rhein.

   Is Cologne on the Rhine?
   Yes, Cologne is on the Rhine.

4. Ist Köln die größte Stadt am Rhein?
   Ja, Köln ist die größte Stadt am Rhein.

   Is Cologne the largest city on the Rhine?
   Yes, Cologne is the largest city on the Rhine.

5. Spricht Mishiko Deutsch?
   Ja, sie spricht Deutsch.

   Does Mishiko speak German?
   Yes, she speaks German.

6. War Mishiko in Berlin?
   Ja, sie war in Berlin.

   Has Mishiko visited Berlin?
   Yes, she has visited Berlin.

7. Wollen Andreas und Mishiko eine Schiffstour auf dem Rhein machen?
   Ja, sie wollen eine Schiffstour auf dem Rhein machen.

   Do Andreas and Mishiko want to take a boat trip down the Rhine?
   Yes, they want to take a boat tour of the Rhine.

8. Zeigt Andreas das Hotel?
   Ja, er zeigt das Hotel.

   Does Andreas show her the hotel?
   Yes, he does.

CD1 TOP3 Übung 2 / Exercise 2

In the following Exercise you should not answer all questions with "ja". You should decide on the correct answer to use!

B **Beispiel/Example:**

Sprecher: *Kommt Andreas aus Köln?*
Speaker: *Does Andreas come from Cologne?*

Sie: *Ja, er kommt aus Köln.*
You: *Yes, he comes from Cologne.*

Sprecher: *Kommt Mishiko aus Köln?*
Speaker: *Does Mishiko come from Cologne?*

Sie: *Nein, sie kommt nicht aus Köln.*
You: *No, she doesn't come from Cologne.*

Exercise:

1. Kommt Andreas aus Köln?   Does Andreas come from Cologne?
Ja, er kommt aus Köln.   *Yes, he comes from Cologne.*

2. Kommt Mishiko aus Köln?   Does Mishiko comes from Cologne?
Nein, sie kommt nicht aus Köln.   *No, she doesn't come from Cologne.*

3. Ist Mishiko das erste Mal in Deutschland?   Is this Mishiko's first visit to Germany?
Nein, sie ist nicht das erste Mal in Deutschland.   *No, this is not her first visit to Germany.*

4. Ist Tokio die größte Stadt am Rhein?   Is Tokyo the largest city on the Rhine?
Nein, Tokio ist nicht die größte Stadt am Rhein.   *No, Tokyo is not the largest city on the Rhine.*

5. Sprechen Mishiko und Andreas Deutsch?   Do Mishiko and Andreas speak German?
Ja, sie sprechen Deutsch.   *Yes, they speak German.*

6. Will Andreas Mishiko helfen?   Does Andreas want to help Mishiko?
Ja, er will Mishiko helfen.   *Yes, he wants to help Mishiko.*

7. Sprechen Mishiko und   Do Mishiko and Andreas speak
Andreas spanisch?   Spanish?
Nein, sie sprechen nicht spanisch.   *No, they do not speak Spanish.*

8. War Andreas schon in Japan?   Has Andreas ever visited Japan?
Nein, er war nicht in Japan.   *No, he has never visited Japan.*

Grammatik/Grammar

Geschlecht von Nomen und bestimmter Artikel / *Gender of nouns and the definite article*

Because there are almost no reliable rules that allow you to figure out the correct gender of a noun or its corresponding article, we recommend that you learn the correct gender of the noun along with the word itself. This is the only way to learn to speak German correctly, without mistakes.
In German you must be able to distinguish between three genders of nouns:

masculine	feminine	neutral

Each grammatical gender has its own article.

Nominative

masculine	feminine	neutral

The definite article

der	die	das
der Mann	die Frau	das Kind
der Fluss	die Stadt	das Hotel

The indefinite article

ein	eine	ein
ein Mann	eine Frau	ein Kind
ein Fluss	eine Stadt	ein Hotel

Important point:
You cannot determine the correct gender of a noun from the meaning of the word. Always learn nouns and the correct gender together.

Konjugation der Verben im Präsens /
Conjugation of Verbs in present tense

First the two auxiliars verbs "sein" and "haben". These verbs are as important in German as they are in most languages.

Sein /

ich bin	wir sind
du bist	ihr seid
er/sie/es ist	sie/Sie sind

haben /

ich habe	wir haben
du hast	ihr habt
er/sie/es hat	sie/Sie haben

kommen /

ich komme	wir kommen
du kommst	ihr kommt
er/sie/es kommt	sie/Sie kommen

The conjugation of verbs in present tense is very predictable. With the verb "kommen" you can see the pattern of the endings. Almost all verbs are conjugated in the same manner.

Hinweise / Situations

Sich begrüßen / Greetings

In German, the greeting depends on the time of day. You should follow the following guidelines:

Until noon, you say "Guten Morgen";

From noon to 5 p.m. you say "Guten Tag";

After 5 p.m. you say "Guten Abend"

Vorsicht! / Attention!

The expression "Gute Nacht" is not a form of greeting!
You should say "Gute Nacht" when you are saying your goodbyes late at night.
You may also say "Gute Nacht" before someone wants to go to sleep.

Friends and acquaintances often greet each other with "Hallo";
this is especially popular with young people.

If you are greeted with "Wie geht's?" or "Wie geht es Ihnen?", your conversation partner is not demanding a direct answer (and definitely not an honest one).
You don't have to go into specifics; simply say "Gut". Only among very good friends do people give a detailed and honest answer.
The same is also true when you ask this question: do not expect a completely truthful answer.

In most cases you say goodbye by saying "Auf Wiedersehen".
By using this phrase there is no chance of making a mistake.
The word "Tschüss" has recently become more popular.
Even though it is really a slang expression, it can be used in most situations.
Along with these greetings and farewells there are also regional differences, but these are not absolutely necessary to learn.
The next chapter contains more specific information on personal forms of address and greetings.

Höflichkeitsformen / Polite forms

When you are seeking help from others or want to ask somebody about something, it is important that you use certain polite phrases along with your question. Immediately after approaching a person, you should say "Entschuldigung" (You can often leave out the greeting, but not the word "Entschuldigung").
If you add an additional "Bitte" after this, then you have put things perfectly.

A few examples:

Guten Tag. Entschuldigung, können Sie mir bitte sagen, wie ich zum Bahnhof komme? (Excuse me, can you tell how to get to the train station?)

or

Entschuldigung. Können Sie mir bitte sagen, wie ich zum Bahnhof komme?

or

Entschuldigen Sie bitte, können Sie mir sagen, wie ich zum Bahnhof komme?

As you can see, the word "Entschuldigung" also can be used as the verb "entschuldigen".
When you have received the desired help or information, or your conversation partner cannot help you any further, say goodbye by using the word "Danke" or "Dankeschön".

Vorsicht! / Attention!

"Entschuldigung" also has another meaning.
In the above example sentences this is only an expression of politeness – without any additional meaning. In other situations this is a way for you to show that you have done something wrong. When you for example, have stepped on somebody's foot, you can also say "Entschuldigung", but now it means "Verzeihung" (forgive me) or "Tut mir Leid" (I'm sorry).

17

Schriftliche Übungen / Written exercises

Insert the correct verb form:

B Beispiel/Example:

Exercise: Entschuldigung, wie _____ ich zum Bahnhof? (kommen)
Solution: Entschuldigung, wie komme ich zum Bahnhof?

Ich _____ seit zwei Wochen in Deutschland. (sein)

Wir _____ seit zwei Wochen in Deutschland. (sein)

Wie _____ Sie bitte? (heißen)

Er _____ Markus Schulz. (heißen)

_____ ihr aus Bayern? (kommen)

Nein, wir _____ aus Hamburg. (kommen)

_____ du heute Zeit? (haben)

Nein, ich _____ leider keine Zeit. (haben)

Mishiko und Andreas _____ Deutsch. (sprechen)

Fragen und Antworten / Questions and answers

Put the questions with the correct answers:

Fragen / Questions	*Antworten* / Answers
Hast du heute Zeit?	1) Nein, ich spreche Spanisch.
Sprichst du Deutsch?	2) Ja, bitte.
Wie heißen Sie?	3) Nein, ich muss zum Arzt.
Kennen Sie Bayern?	4) Nein, sie kommt aus Tokio.
Ist Köln eine Stadt am Rhein?	5) Meine Name ist Andreas.
Soll ich die Fahrkarten kaufen?	6) Nein, dort war ich noch nicht.
Kommt Mishiko aus Madrid?	7) Ja, es ist die größte Stadt.

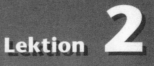

Lektion 2

Freunde treffen und Fremden begegnen

CD1
TOP5 Freunde treffen und Fremden begegnen /
Meeting friends and introducing yourself to people

As you saw in the previous lesson, certain patterns of behaviour are included in greetings. In this lesson you can read and hear how to behave when you greet friends or make new acquaintances.
You will learn:

– Forms of addressing friends and acquaintances;
– Forms of addressing your employers and new acquaintances;
– Differences between polite and casual ways of speaking.

Wichtige Formulierungen! / Important forms of addressing people!
First, listen to these phrases:

Schön, dass du hier bist.	Nice to see you.
Darf ich dir meinen Kollegen vorstellen?	May I introduce you to my colleagues? (informal)
Darf ich Ihnen meinen Kollegen vorstellen?	May I introduce you to my colleagues? (formal)
Sehr erfreut.	Pleased to meet you.
Ich freue mich, dich zu sehen.	Good to see you.
Ich freue mich, Sie zu sehen.	I'm happy to see you.
Ich freue mich auch.	Me, too.
Hast du heute Abend Zeit?	Are you free this evening?
Haben Sie heute Abend Zeit?	Would you be free this evening?
Sollen wir uns für morgen verabreden?	Should we meet again tomorrow?
Ja, morgen passt mir sehr gut.	Yes, tomorrow suits me fine.
Nein, morgen passt mir gar nicht.	No, I'm afraid I can't make it tomorrow.
Darf ich Sie zum Essen einladen?	Could I invite you to dine with me?
Ich hole dich morgen um 19:00 Uhr ab.	I'll pick you up at 7:00 tomorrow evening
Ich hole Sie morgen um 19:00 Uhr ab.	Yes sir, I'll pick you up at 7:00 tomorrow evening.
Es war mir ein Vergnügen.	It was my pleasure.

Dialogue 2

Now listen to the following dialogue.

Andreas:
Hallo Mishiko! Schön, dass du hier bist.

Mishiko:
Hallo Andreas! Ich freue mich auch.
Wie geht es dir?

Andreas:
Danke gut. Darf ich dir meinen
neuen Kollegen vorstellen?
Das ist Herr Thöne. Herr Thöne, das
ist Frau Thai.

Mishiko:
Guten Tag Herr Thöne. Ich freue mich,
Sie kennen zu lernen.

Herr Thöne:
Guten Tag Frau Thai. Es ist mir ein
Vergnügen, Ihre Bekanntschaft
zu machen.

Andreas:
Mishiko, hast du heute Abend Zeit,
dann können wir gemeinsam etwas
unternehmen.

Mishiko:
Nein, tut mit Leid. Heute Abend habe
ich schon etwas vor. Aber wie wäre es
mit morgen Abend?

Andreas:
Morgen Abend würde mir auch passen.
Herr Thöne, hätten Sie morgen
Abend auch Zeit?

Herr Thöne:
Ja, morgen Abend passt mir sehr gut.
Um wie viel Uhr sollen wir uns
denn treffen?

Andreas:
Hello Mishiko, good to see you.

Mishiko:
Hello Andreas! Good to see you, too.
How are you?

Andreas:
Fine, thanks. Can I introduce you to a new
colleague of mine? This is Mr. Thöne,
Mr. Thöne, this is Miss Thai.

Mishiko:
Hello Mr. Thöne, pleased to meet you.

Mr. Thöne:
Hello Miss Thai. I am pleased
to meet you.

Andreas:
Mishiko, if you have time tonight, we
could do something together.

Mishiko:
I'm sorry, but I already have plans tonight.
How about tomorrow evening?

Andreas:
Tomorrow evening would suit me fine.
Mr. Thöne, would tomorrow evening suit you?

Mr. Thöne:
Yes, tomorrow evening would suit me fine.
What time should we meet?

Mishiko:
Bitte nicht zu früh. Ich schlage
19:00 Uhr vor.

Andreas:
Gut. Dann holen wir dich um 19:00
Uhr zu Hause ab.

Mishiko:
Ja, das wäre sehr nett.

Herr Thöne:
Frau Thai, darf ich Sie zum Essen
einladen?

Mishiko:
Danke, sehr gerne.

Andreas:
Schön, dann bis morgen um 19:00 Uhr.
Tschüss.

Herr Thöne:
Frau Thai, es war mir ein Vergnügen,
Sie kennen gelernt zu haben.
Auf Wiedersehen.

Mishiko:
Danke. Auf Wiedersehen.

Mishiko:
Please, not too early. I suggest 7:00 p.m.

Andreas:
Great. Then we'll pick you up at your
door at 7 p.m. Is that o.k.?

Mishiko:
Yes, that would be very nice.

Mr. Thöne:
Miss Thai, could I invite you to dinner?

Mishiko:
Yes, thank you very much.

Andreas:
Great. Then, until tomorrow at 7 p.m.
Goodbye.

Mr. Thöne:
Miss Thai, it was a pleasure to meet you.

Goodbye.

Mishiko:
Thank you. Goodbye.

I recommend that you listen to the entire dialogue one more time. You should also repeat the individual sentences so that you can get the right feeling for the correct pronunciation.
(If the dialogue is too fast, please use the pause button on your CD player.)

Übung 1 / Exercise 1:

In this exercise you should familiarise yourself with the different ways of addressing people. Always keep in mind that you always address people you don't know with the polite form of address "Sie". You should only use "du" with people who address you first with "du".

B Beispiel / Example:

Sprecher:	*Guten Tag Frau Thai. Haben Sie einen Moment Zeit für mich?*
Speaker:	*Hello, Miss Thai. Do you have a minute?*
Sie:	*Ja, ich habe einen Moment Zeit für Sie.*
You:	*Yes, I have a moment.*
Sprecher:	*Hallo Mishiko, hast du einen Moment Zeit für mich?*
Speaker:	*Hello, Mishiko, do you have a minute?*
Sie:	*Ja, ich habe einen Moment Zeit für dich.*
You:	*Yes, I have a minute.*
Sprecher:	*Guten Morgen Herr und Frau Niepmann. Darf ich Sie ein Stück begleiten?*
Speaker:	*Good morning, Mr. and Mrs. Niepmann. Could I join you?*
Sie:	*Guten Morgen! Ja, Sie dürfen uns ein Stück begleiten.*
You:	*Good morning. Yes, you can.*
Sprecher:	*Guten Abend Mishiko und Andreas, darf ich euch ein Stück begleiten?*
Speaker:	*Hello Mishiko and Andreas, can I join you?*
Sie:	*Ja, du darfst uns ein Stück begleiten.*
You:	*Sure! Come along!*

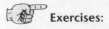 **Exercises:**

Answer the following questions with "ja".

1. Guten Tag Sabine. Kommst du
   mich heute besuchen?
   Ja, ich komme dich heute besuchen.

   Hello Sabine. Do you want to drop
   by today?
   Yes, I can come by.

2. Guten Tag Herr Alberts. Kommen
   Sie mich heute besuchen?
   Ja, ich komme Sie heute besuchen.

   Hello Mr. Alberts. Could you come by
   for a visit today?
   Yes, I could.

3. Können wir uns heute Mittag
   treffen?
   *Ja, wir können uns heute
   Mittag treffen.*

   Could we meet at noon?

   Yes, that would be fine.

4. Hallo Frank und Thomas.
   Könnt ihr gleich zu mir kommen?
   *Ja, wir können gleich zu dir
   kommen.*

   Hello Frank and Thomas, do you want
   to drop by now?
   Yes, we can do that.

5. Guten Abend Herr und
   Frau Fuhrmann. Können Sie gleich
   zu mir kommen?
   *Ja, wir können gleich zu Ihnen
   kommen.*

   Good evening Mr. and Mrs. Fuhrmann.
   Could you stop by now for a visit?

   Yes, that would be fine.

Übung 2 / Exercise 2:

In this exercise you should familiarise yourself with the conjugation of verbs in the present tense. Create sentences using all the personal pronoun forms. Please keep in mind that some verbs have some spelling differences (a change of vowel) even in the present tense The verb list in the appendix will show you which verbs these are.

B **Beispiel / Example:**

Sprecher: *nach Hause kommen*
Speaker: *to come home*

Sie: *Ich komme nach Hause.*
You: *I am coming home.*

Du kommst nach Hause.

You are coming home. (informal)

Er kommt nach Hause.

He is coming home.

Sie kommt nach Hause.

She is coming home.

Es kommt nach Hause.

It is coming home.

Wir kommen nach Hause.

We are coming home.

Ihr kommt nach Hause.

You are coming home. (informal plural)

Sie kommen nach Hause.

They are coming home.

Sprecher:	*mit einem Freund sprechen*
Speaker:	*to speak with a friend*
Sie:	*Ich spreche mit einem Freund.*
You:	*I am speaking with a friend.*

Du sprichst mit einem Freund.

You are speaking with a friend. (informal)

Er spricht mit einem Freund.

He is speaking with a friend.

Sie spricht mit einem Freund.

She is speaking with a friend.

Es spricht mit einem Freund.

It is speaking with a friend.

Wir sprechen mit einem Freund.

We are speaking with a friend.

Ihr sprecht mit einem Freund.

You are speaking with a friend. (informal plural)

Sie sprechen mit einem Freund.

They are speaking with a friend.

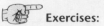 **Exercises:**

1. eine Bekanntschaft machen
Ich mache eine Bekanntschaft.
Du machst eine Bekanntschaft.

Er macht eine Bekanntschaft.
Sie macht eine Bekanntschaft.
Es macht eine Bekanntschaft.
Wir machen eine Bekanntschaft.
Ihr macht eine Bekanntschaft.

Sie machen eine Bekanntschaft.

to make a new acquaintance
I am making a new acquaintance.
You are making a new acquaintance.
(informal singular)
He is making a new acquaintance.
She is making a new acquaintance.
It is making a new acquaintance.
We are making a new acquaintance.
You are making a new acquaintance.
(informal plural)
They are making a new acquaintance.

2. einkaufen gehen
Ich gehe einkaufen.
Du gehst einkaufen.
Er geht einkaufen.
Sie geht einkaufen.
Es geht einkaufen.
Wir gehen einkaufen.
Ihr geht einkaufen.
Sie gehen einkaufen.

to shop
I am shopping.
You are shopping. (informal)
He is shopping.
She is shopping.
It is shopping.
We are shopping.
You are shopping. (informal plural)
They are shopping.

3. eine Freundin sehen
Ich sehe eine Freundin.
Du siehst eine Freundin.
Er sieht eine Freundin.
Sie sieht eine Freundin.
Es sieht eine Freundin.
Wir sehen eine Freundin.
Ihr seht eine Freundin.
Sie sehen eine Freundin.

to visit a friend
I am visiting a friend.
You are visiting a friend. (informal)
He is visiting a friend.
She is visiting a friend.
It is visiting a friend.
We are visiting a friend.
You are visiting a friend. (informal plural)
They are visiting a friend.

Übung 3 / Exercise 3:

In the following exercises you should first answer the questions with "ja" and then with "nein".

B **Beispiel / Example:**

Sprecher: *Sind Sie schon lange in Deutschland?*
Speaker: *Have you been in Germany long?*

Sie: *Ja, ich bin schon lange in Deutschland.*
You: *Yes, I have been here for a while.*
Nein, ich bin nicht lange in Deutschland. No, I haven't been in Germany for long.

Sprecher: *Kennen Sie Frau Fuhrmann?*
Speaker: *Do you already know Mrs. Fuhrmann?*

Sie: *Ja, ich kenne Frau Fuhrmann.*
You: *I know Mrs. Fuhrmann.*
Nein, ich kenne Frau Fuhrmann nicht.
No I don't know Mrs. Fuhrmann.

Exercises:

1. Haben Sie heute Abend Zeit für mich?
   Do you have some time for me this evening?
   Ja, ich habe heute Abend Zeit für Sie.
   Yes, I have time this evening.
   Nein, ich habe heute Abend keine Zeit für Sie.
   No, I don't have time this evening.

2. Haben Sie meinen Kollegen kennen gelernt?
   Have you met my colleague yet?
   Ja, ich habe Ihren Kollegen kennen gelernt.
   Yes, I have met your colleague.
   Nein, ich habe Ihren Kollgen nicht kennen gelernt.
   No, I haven't met your colleague.

3. Soll ich dich morgen abholen?   Should I pick you up tomorrow?
    Ja, du sollst mich morgen   *Yes, that would be fine.*
    abholen.
    Nein, du sollst mich morgen   *No thanks, I don't need a ride tomorrow.*
    nicht abholen.

4. Gehen wir ins Kino?   Are we going to the cinema?
    Ja, wir gehen ins Kino.   *Yes, we are going to the cinema.*
    Nein, wir gehen nicht ins Kino.   *No, we aren't going to the cinema.*

5. Besuchen wir unseren Freund?   Are we visiting our friend?
    Ja, wir besuchen unseren Freund.   *Yes, we are visiting our friend.*
    Nein, wir besuchen nicht   *No, we are not visiting our friend.*
    unseren Freund.

6. Hast du ein Auto?   Do you have a car?
    Ja, ich habe ein Auto.   *Yes, I have a car.*
    Nein, ich habe kein Auto.   *No, I don't have a car.*

7. Fahren wir mit dem Auto   Are we taking the car along the Rhine?
    an den Rhein?
    Ja, wir fahren mit dem Auto   *Yes, we are driving along the Rhine.*
    an den Rhein.
    Nein, wir fahren nicht mit dem   *No, we are not driving along the Rhine.*
    Auto an den Rhein.

8. Hat Ihnen das Konzert gut gefallen?   Did you like the concert?
    Ja, das Konzert hat mir gut gefallen.   *Yes, I liked the concert.*
    Nein, das Konzert hat mir nicht   *No, I didn't like the concert.*
    gut gefallen.

9. Möchten Sie ein Glas Wein trinken?   Would you like a glass of wine?
    Ja, ich möchte ein Glas   *Yes, a glass of wine would be fine.*
    Wein trinken.
    Nein, ich möchte kein Glas   *No, thank you.*
    Wein trinken.

10. Siehst du dort das Restaurant?   Do you see that restaurant there?
    Ja, ich sehe dort das Restaurant.   *Yes, I see the restaurant.*
    Nein, ich sehe dort kein Restaurant.   *No, I don't see any restaurant.*

Grammatik / Grammar

Der Plural / The plural

As you have already seen in Lesson 1, the relationship of nouns and gender has almost no system and is quite arbitrary. The same applies to the plural nouns as well. I can only recommend that you learn the plural for each new noun at the same time that you learn its gender.

The following table gives an overview of the possible plural endings.

	-	-e	-en	-er
Singular	das Fenster	der Riss	die Frau	das Kind
Plural	die Fenster	die Risse	die Frauen	die Kinder

	- n	-s	-e	-er
Singular	die Tasche	das Auto	der Bach	das Rad
Plural	die Taschen	die Autos	die Bäche	die Räder

	-er		
Singular	der Mann		
Plural	die Männer		

As you can see, the number of possible plural endings is quite large.
Additionally, there are also many nouns that either have only a singular form or only a plural form. Because this problem exists in almost every language, we will not go into this subject further.

Konjugation schwieriger Verben im Präsens / Conjugation of difficult verbs in present tense
For the most part, the conjugation of verbs in the present tense is very systematic and creates few problems.

You should, however, pay additional attention to some particular verbs because they change vowels in the second and third person singular.

	sprechen	sehen	werden	stehlen
ich	spreche	sehe	werde	stehle
du	sprichst	siehst	wirst	stiehlst
er/sie/es	spricht	sieht	wird	stiehlt
wir	sprechen	sehen	werden	stehlen
ihr	sprecht	seht	werdet	stehlt
sie/Sie	sprechen	sehen	werden	stehlen

This list is not comprehensive.

It also makes sense here to learn verbs by heart because you will use them quite frequently.

Hinweis / Tip :

The present tense is a very important grammar form in German. With this form you can create any sentence that expresses present as well as future situations.
The temporal adjective in the sentence tells you the time frame. You do not need to add any additional time indicator.

Example:

Heute gehe ich in die Stadt.

Morgen gehe ich in die Stadt.

As you can see, the grammatical form of each sentence is the same. Only the words "heute" and "morgen" define the time.

Die Höflichkeitsform mit "Sie" / The polite form of address with "Sie"

In the German language the personal pronoun *"Sie"* has many meanings that you should be able to discern.

"Sie" can in be used in third person singular to stand for feminine nouns. In this case it is always conjugated in the singular.

Beispiel / Example:

Die Frau geht in den Garten.   Sie geht in den Garten.

"Sie" can also stand for the third person plural. In this case you must distinguish between several possibilities.

a) *"Sie"* is a personal pronoun for plural nouns. Here you must write *"sie"* in lower case. The conjugation is singular.

b) *"Sie"* is a personal pronoun used for politely addressing an individual formally. Here you must capitalise *"Sie"*. The conjugation is plural.

c) *"Sie"* is a personal pronoun to formally address a group of people. Here you must capitalise *"Sie"*. The conjugation is plural.

Beispiel / Example:

to a) *Spielen die Kinder im Garten?*
Spielen sie im Garten?

to b) *Herr Müller, kommen Sie bitte in das Büro.*

to c) *Herr und Frau Müller, kommen Sie bitte in das Büro.*

Hinweis / Important:

Always be sure to conjugate the verb in the plural, when you use the polite forms of address, even when you are only speaking to one person.

Der Akkusativ / The accusative case

In German the verbs determine the case forms. In most cases the verbs take both a nominative and an accusative case. When you put a masculine noun in the accusative case, the article changes. With feminine and neuter nouns the article does not change.

Beispiel / Example:

| Ich frage den Mann. | Ich frage die Frau. | Ich frage das Kind. |

With masculine nouns the article always changes from *"der"* to *"den"*.

The same is also true when the accusative is represented by a personal pronoun. In the feminine and neuter forms this is the same as the nominative. Masculine forms change from "er" to "ihn".

Beispiel / Exemples:

| Ich frage ihn. | Ich frage sie. | Ich frage es. |

Hinweise / Situation

Die Anredeformen / The correct forms of address

In the grammar section of this lesson you have already seen that there are different forms for addressing people in German.
Here I would like to show you when you should use each form, in order to be polite during a conversation with Germans.

In principle you should address new acquaintances with *"Sie"*. This form of address is appropriate for any situation. *"Sie"* also means that you should address your conversation partner by name with *"Herr"* or *"Frau"*.
Only the people that address you with *"du"* should be addressed in the same manner. Of course you will also have the opportunity to address somebody with this more intimate form of address; but you should not forget a couple of rules:

– Older people address younger people with "du";
– Superiors in a company address their subordinates with "du".

Even though Germans often ignore these rules, it is advisable to follow the rules. These rituals are often difficult for outsiders to comprehend and may lead to conflicts if not followed correctly.

Children up to the age of 16 can be addressed with *"du"*.

Young people do not adhere so strictly to this procedure any more. In many cases you will here *"du"* immediately after the first contact with a person.

The polite *"Sie"* is however always used in letters and capitalised, while *"du"* is not. This is also true for the declination of the personal pronouns.

Alltagssprache und Hochsprache / Everyday speech and formal speech

There is hardly another language where the distinction between the written and the spoken language is so large as it is in German.
While the written language follows only the grammar rules of High German, the everyday speech often goes sharply against these rules.
Also in these situations it is often very difficult to recognise which rules can be bent and which cannot. The situation you are in determines the qualities and level of the language used.
However, if you limit yourself to using High German, you can hardly go wrong.
You should only try out the everyday idioms and expressions you have learnt when you are among friends.
When writing, it is advisable that you use only High German.

Schriftliche Übungen / Written exercises

Please insert the correct personal pronoun.

a) Frau Hellmann, kommen _____ bitte zu mir.

b) Siehst du das Mädchen dort? Ja, ich sehe _____.

c) Kennen Sie Herrn und Frau Thöne? Nein, ich kenne _____ nicht.

d) Klaus, kannst _____ in der Stadt etwas einkaufen?

e) Hallo Klaus und Sabrina. Sollen _____ zusammen ins Kino gehen?

f) Guten Tagen Petra und Felix. Habt _____ euch ein neues Auto ge-kauft?

g) Herr Hammel, haben Sie gleich etwas Zeit? Ja, _____ habe gleich etwas Zeit.

h) Dort geht Wolfgang. Hast _____ ihn auch gesehen?

Please insert the correct plural form.

	Singular	Plural	
a)	das Kind	die	_____
b)	die Frau	die	_____
c)	der Mann	die	_____
d)	die Straße	die	_____
e)	der Herr	die	_____
f)	das Radio	die	_____
g)	der Mensch	die	_____
h)	das Kino	die	_____
i)	die Stadt	die	_____
j)	das Land	die	_____
k)	der Freund	die	_____
l)	die Freundin	die	_____
m)	der Kollege	die	_____
n)	der Zucker	die	_____

Mit der Bahn verreisen

CD1
TOP10 In this lesson you will learn and practise how you can use the public transport system in Germany (especially the train). In addition to the information necessary to help you in these situations, I will also familiarise you with typical conditions on the trains here in Germany.

You will learn:

- How to ask for information;
- How you can buy train tickets;
- The most important facts about travel in Germany.

Wichtige Formulierungen! / Important phrases!

First listen to these sentences:

Wie komme ich am schnellsten von Wuppertal nach München?	What is the quickest route from Wuppertal to Munich?
Wann fährt der nächste Zug nach München?	When does the next train leave for Munich?
Muss ich umsteigen?	Do I have to change trains?
Wie oft muss ich umsteigen?	How often do I have to change trains?
Wo muss ich umsteigen?	Where do I have to change trains?
Ich hätte gerne eine Fahrkarte von Wuppertal nach München.	I would like a ticket from Wuppertal to Munich, please.
Einfache Fahrt. Hin- und Rückfahrt.	One way ticket. Round trip ticket.
Fährt der Zug über Köln?	Does the train go through Cologne?
Wie teuer ist eine Fahrkarte von Wuppertal nach München?	How much does a ticket from Wuppertal to Munich cost?
Darf ich mit dieser Karte auch den ICE benutzen?	Can I take an Intercity Express train with this ticket?

Ich möchte gerne einen Fensterplatz reservieren.	I would like to reserve a window seat.
Wann kommt der Zug in München an?	When does the train arrive in Munich?
Habe ich in Mannheim einen guten Anschluss?	Is there a good connection in Mannheim?
Gibt es in diesem Zug ein Restaurant?	Is there a restaurant car on this train?
Kann ich eine Ermäßigung bekommen?	Can I get a discount price?
Auf welchem Bahnsteig fährt der Zug ab?	Which platform does the train depart from?
Habe ich in München Anschluss an die S-Bahn?	Is there a connection with the commuter train in Munich?
Darf ich in diesem Wagen rauchen?	May I smoke in this carriage?
Ich hätte gerne einen Platz für Nichtraucher.	I would like a seat in a non-smoking section.
Gibt es auch einen Schlafwagen?	Is there also a sleeping car?
Das ist alles.	That's all.

Dialogue 3

Now listen to the following dialogue.

Mishiko wants to travel the day after tomorrow on the train from Wuppertal to Munich. She goes to the Wuppertal main station to get information on the connections and to buy tickets.

Listen to the conversation between Mishiko and the German rail travel agent.

Mishiko:
Guten Tag. Ich möchte gerne übermorgen mit dem Zug von Wuppertal nach München fahren. Können Sie mir bitte einige Verbindungen nennen?

Mishiko:
Hello. I would like to travel from Wuppertal to Munich the day after tomorrow. Could you tell me a few possible connections?

Angestellter:
Guten Tag. Um wie viel Uhr möchten Sie denn ungefähr fahren?

Travel agent:
Hello. And when approximately would you like to depart?

Mishiko:
Ich möchte so gegen 8:00 Uhr morgens fahren, damit ich nicht zu spät in München ankomme.

Mishiko:
I would like to leave at around 8:00 in the morning, so I won't arrive too late in Munich.

Angestellter:
Einen Augenblick bitte. Es fährt ein Zug um 7:42 Uhr. Da müssen Sie aber in Köln und in Mannheim umsteigen. Wenn Sie den Zug um 8:42 Uhr nehmen, müssen Sie nur in Mannheim umsteigen.

Travel agent:
One moment please. There is a train that leaves at 7:42, but you'll have to change trains in Cologne and Mannheim. If you take the 8:42 train, you would only have to change in Mannheim.

Mishiko:
8:42 Uhr passt mir gut. Wann kommt der Zug denn in München an?

Mishiko:
8:42 sounds fine. When does the train arrive in Munich?

Angestellter:
Sie sind dann um 15:00 Uhr in München.

Travel agent:
You arrive at 3 p.m. in Munich.

Mishiko:
Das ist gut. Wie teuer ist denn die Fahrkarte?

Mishiko:
That suits me fine. How much is the ticket?

Angestellter:
Einfache Fahrt?

Travel agent:
One way?

Mishiko:
Nein, Hin- und Rückfahrt bitte.

Mishiko:
No, round trip, please.

Angestellter:
Hin- und Rückfahrt Wuppertal – München
kostet 421 DM.

Travel agent:
Round trip from Wuppertal to Munich
costs 421 Marks.

Mishiko:
Darf ich mit dieser Fahrkarte dann auch
den ICE benutzen?

Mishiko:
Can I take an Inter-City Express train with
this ticket?

Angestellter:
Ja, in Mannheim müssen Sie in einen
ICE umsteigen. Dieser Preis ist
in Ihrer Fahrkarte enthalten.

Travel agent:
Yes, in Mannheim you have to switch to an
ICE train. The surcharge is included in
the ticket.

Mishiko:
Habe ich in Mannheim denn einen guten
Anschluss, oder muss ich dort
länger warten?

Mishiko:
Do I have a good connection in Mannheim or
do I have to wait for a long time?

Angestellter:
Sie haben nur sechs Minuten Aufenthalt
in Mannheim.

Travel agent:
There is only a six-minute wait in Mannheim.

Mishiko:
Gut. Dann hätte ich gern diese Fahrkarte.

Mishiko:
Good. I'll buy the ticket, then.

Angestellter:
Möchten Sie auch eine
Platzreservierung vornehmen?

Travel agent:
Would you also like to reserve a seat?

Mishiko:
Ja bitte. Ich möchte einen Platz im
Raucherabteil. Bitte am Fenster.

Mishiko:
Yes, please. I would like a seat in the smoking
section, a window seat.

Angestellter:
Großraumwagen oder Abteilwagen?

Travel agent:
And do you want to be in an open or
closed car?

Mishiko:
Großraumwagen.

Mishiko:
An open car, please.

Angestellter:	*Travel agent:*
Gut, ich habe einen Platz im Großraumwagen, Raucher, Fenster für Sie reserviert.	Right. You have a reserved seat in an open car, the smoking section, and it's a window seat.
Mishiko:	*Mishiko:*
Gibt es in diesem Zug auch ein Restaurant?	Is there an on-board restaurant on the train?
Angestellter:	*Travel agent:*
Selbstverständlich gibt es ein Zugrestaurant.	Certainly.
Mishiko:	*Mishiko:*
Kann ich eine Ermäßigung auf diesen Fahrpreis bekommen?	Is there a discount price available for this price?
Angestellter:	*Travel agent:*
Eine Ermäßigung gibt es nur, wenn Sie eine Bahncard haben. Dann müssen Sie nur den halben Fahrpreis bezahlen.	There is only a discount when you have a Bahncard, which means you pay only half price.
Mishiko:	*Mishiko:*
Schade, aber eine Bahncard habe ich leider nicht.	Unfortunately I don't have a Bahncard.
Angestellter:	*Travel agent:*
So, das macht dann zusammen 424 DM.	Right. Altogether, that is 424 Marks.
Mishiko:	*Mishiko:*
Kann ich auch mit der Eurocard bezahlen?	Can I pay with my Eurocard?
Angestellter:	*Travel agent:*
Selbstverständlich.	Certainly.
Mishiko:	*Mishiko:*
Schönen Dank. Auf Wiedersehen.	Thank you. Good bye.
Angestellter:	*Travel agent:*
Auf Wiedersehen.	Good bye!

I recommend that you listen to the entire dialogue one more time. You should also repeat the individual sentences so that you can get the right feeling for the correct pronunciation.
(If the dialogue is too fast, please use the pause button on your CD player.)

Übung 1/Exercise 1:

In the following exercise you can practise the different interrogative pronouns. You will first hear a statement. Ask a question after the first part of this statement.

B Beispiel/Examples:

Sprecher:	*Um 13:15 Uhr fährt der Zug nach München.*	
Speaker:	*The train to Munich leaves at 1:15 p.m.*	1.
		2.
Sie:	*Wann fährt der Zug nach München?*	3.
You:	*When does the train to Munich leave?*	

Sprecher: *Dort fährt der Zug nach München.*
Speaker: *The train to Munich leaves from there.*

Sie: *Wo fährt der Zug nach München?*
You: *Where does the train to Munich leave from?*

 Exercises:

1. Mishiko fährt nach München. Mishiko is travelling to Munich.
 Wer fährt nach München? *Who is travelling to Munich?*

2. Nach München fährt Mishiko. Mishiko is travelling to Munich.
 Wohin fährt Mishiko? *Where is Mishiko travelling?*

3. Ihren Freund besucht Mishiko. She is visiting her friend.
 Wen besucht Mishiko? *Who is Mishiko visiting?*

4. Auf Gleis 3 steht der Zug
   nach München.
   Wo steht der Zug nach München?

   The train to Munich departs from
   platform 3.
   Where does the train to Munich leave?

5. In der Stadt gehen Mishiko
   und Andreas spazieren.
   ***Wo gehen Mishiko und Andreas
   spazieren?***

   Mishiko and Andreas are walking in
   the city.
   ***Where are Mishiko and Andreas
   walking?***

6. In die Schule gehen die Kinder
   jeden Morgen.
   ***Wohin gehen die Kinder jeden
   Morgen?***

   The children go to school every morning.

   Where do the children go every morning?

7. Um 18:00 Uhr isst die Familie
   zu Abend.
   Wann isst die Familie zu Abend?

   The family eats dinner at 6 p.m.

   When does the family eat dinner?

8. In dem Kleiderschrank hängen
   Mishikos Jacken.
   Wo hängen Mishikos Jacken?

   Mishiko's jackets are hanging in the
   wardrobe.
   Where are Mishiko's jackets?

9. In den Kleiderschrank hängt
   Mishiko ihre Jacken.
   Wohin hängt Mishiko ihre Jacken?

   Mishiko hangs her jackets in the
   wardrobe.
   Where does Mishiko hang her jackets?

10. Alle Züge nach München
    fahren über Köln.
    Was fährt nach Köln?

    All trains to Munich go through
    Cologne.
    Which trains go through Cologne?

11. Einen Ring schenkt der Mann
    seiner Frau zum Geburtstag.
    ***Was schenkt der Mann seiner
    Frau zum Geburtstag?***

    The man is giving his wife a ring for her
    birthday.
    ***What is the man giving his wife for
    her birthday?***

12. Jeden Abend sieht er die
    Nachrichten im Fernsehen.
    ***Wann sieht er die Nachrichten
    im Fernsehen?***

    Every evening, he watches the news on
    television.
    ***When does he watch the news on
    television?***

13. Im Fernsehen sieht er jeden
    Abend die Nachrichten.
    ***Wo sieht er jeden Abend
    die Nachrichten?***

    He watches the news every night on
    television.
    ***Where does he watch the news every
    night?***

14. Auf den Sessel setzt sie sich,
um sich auszuruhen.
Wohin setzt sie sich, um
sich auszuruhen?

She is sitting on the couch to relax.
Where does he sit when he wants
to relax?

15. Auf diesem Stuhl sitzt Andreas.
Wo sitzt Andreas?

Andreas is sitting on this chair.
Where is Andreas sitting?

16. Das Auto steht abends
in der Garage.
Wo steht das Auto abends?

The car is parked in the garage at night.

Where is the car parked at night?

17. Die Reisenden nehmen den
Zug um 8:42 Uhr.
Wer nimmt den Zug um 8:42 Uhr?

The travellers are taking the train at
8:42 a.m.
Who is taking the train at 8:42 a.m.?

D1 Übung 2/Exercise 2:
P13
Now you will practise the times of day in German.
The speaker will give you the times in the digital form.

B Beispiel/Example

Sprecher: *Der Zug kommt um 8:15 Uhr in*
München an.
Speaker: *The train arrives in Munich at 8:15 a.m.*

Sie: *Der Zug kommt um Viertel nach*
acht in München an.
You: *The train arrives in Munich at a quarter*
past eight.

Sprecher: *Ich komme um 7:25 Uhr zu dir.*
Speaker: *I am coming to yours at 7:25 a.m.*

Sie: *Ich komme um fünf vor halb acht zu dir.*
You: *I am coming to yours at twenty-five past eight.*

● 1.
● 2.
● 3.

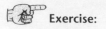 **Exercise:**

1. Um 11:10 Uhr besucht Andreas
seine Bekannte.
Um zehn nach elf besucht Andreas
seine Bekannte.

At 11:10 Andreas is visiting his friends.
At ten after eleven Andreas is visiting
his friends.

2. Wir besuchen euch morgen
um 7:15 Uhr.
Wir besuchen euch morgen um
Viertel nach sieben.

We will visit you tomorrow at 7:15 a.m.
We will visit you tomorrow at a quarter
past seven.

3. Der Zug fährt um 9:30 Uhr in
Wuppertal ab.
Der Zug fährt um halb zehn
in Wuppertal ab.

The train leaves Wuppertal at 9:30 a.m.
The train leaves Wuppertal at half past
nine.

4. Viele Geschäfte schließen in
Deutschland um 18:30 Uhr.
Viele Geschäfte schließen in
Deutschland um halb sieben.

Many businesses in Germany close at
6:30 p.m.
Many businesses in Germany close at a
half past six in the evening.

5. Herr Schulte geht jeden Morgen
um 8:25 Uhr aus dem Haus.
Herr Schulte geht jeden Morgen um
fünf vor halb neun aus dem Haus.

Mr Schulte leaves home at 8:25 every
morning.
Mr Schulte leaves home at twenty-five
past eight every morning.

6. Sollen wir am Mittwoch um
17:45 Uhr ins Kino gehen?
Sollen wir am Mittwoch um
Viertel vor sechs ins Kino gehen?

Should we go to the cinema on
Wednesday at 5:45 p.m.?
Should we go to the cinema on
Wednesday at a quarter to six?

7. Der Zug erreicht Köln
um 21:35 Uhr.
Der Zug erreicht Köln um
fünf nach halb zehn.

The train arrives in Cologne at 9:35 p.m.
The train arrives in Cologne at twenty-
five to ten.

8. Sie hat um 23:20 Uhr
eine Verabredung.
Sie hat um zwanzig nach
elf eine Verabredung.

She has an appointment at 11:20 p.m.
She has an appointment at twenty
past eleven at night.

9. Mishiko kam gestern Abend
erst um 22:50 Uhr nach Hause.
Mishiko kam gestern Abend
erst um zehn vor elf nach Hause.

Mishiko came home yesterday evening
at 10:50 p.m.
Mishiko came home yesterday evening
at ten to eleven.

10. Sie müssen um 23:59 Uhr in
Mannheim umsteigen.
Sie müssen um eine Minute
vor zwölf in Mannheim umsteigen.

You have to change trains in Mannheim
at 11:59 p.m.
You have to change trains in Mannheim
at one minute to twelve.

11. Der Intercity fährt um
12:01 Uhr in Bonn ab.
Der Intercity fährt um eine
Minute nach zwölf in Bonn ab.

The Intercity departs Bonn at 12:01 p.m.

The Intercity departs Bonn at one
minute past noon.

12. Der Spielfilm im Fernsehen
beginnt um 20:27 Uhr.
Der Spielfilm im Fernsehen beginnt
um 3 Minuten vor halb neun.

The movie on television begins at
8:27 p.m.
The movie on television begins at
twenty-seven past eight in the evening.

13. Um 19:37 Uhr war das
Fußballspiel zu Ende.
Um sieben Minuten nach halb
acht war das Fußballspiel zu Ende.

The football match ended at 7:37 p.m.

The football match ended at thirty-
seven past seven.

14. Andreas muß um 6:51 Uhr
umsteigen.
Andreas muss um neun
Minuten vor sieben umsteigen.

Andreas will have to change trains
at 6:51 a.m.
Andreas will have to change trains
at nine minutes to seven.

Übung 3/Exercise 3:

Here you should use the personal pronouns in the dative and accusative cases.
Replace the people in the following sentences with the appropriate pronouns.

B Beispiel/Example

Sprecher: *Er fragt den Angestellten nach der Uhrzeit.*
Speaker: *He is asking the travel agent for the time.*

Sie: *Er fragt ihn nach der Uhrzeit.*
You: *He is asking him for the time.*

Sprecher: *Er antwortet der Frau.*
Speaker: *He is answering the lady.*

Sie: *Er antwortet ihr.*
You: *He is answering her.*

Sprecher: *Sie hilft dem Mann in den Zug.*
Speaker: *She is helping the man into the train.*

Sie: *Sie hilft ihm in den Zug.*
You: *She is helping him into the train.*

Exercise:

1. Er fragt den Angestellten
   nach der Uhrzeit.
   Er fragt ihn nach der Uhrzeit.

   He is asking the travel agent for the time.

   He is asking him for the time.

2. Er antwortet der Frau.
   Er antwortet ihr.

   He is answering the lady.
   He is answering her.

3. Sie hilft dem Mann in den Zug.
   Sie hilft ihm in den Zug.

   She is helping the man into the train.
   She is helping him into the train.

4. Der Angestellte gibt der
   Frau eine Auskunft.
   *Der Angestellte gibt ihr
   eine Auskunft.*

   The travel agent is giving the lady
   information.
   *The travel agent is giving her
   information.*

5. Ich begleite die Frau zum Bahnhof.
   Ich begleite sie zum Bahnhof.

   I am accompanying the lady to the station.
   I am accompanying her to the station.

6. Du fährst morgen mit deiner
   Frau nach München.
   *Du fährst morgen mit ihr
   nach München.*

   You are travelling with your wife to
   Munich tomorrow.
   *You are travelling with her to Munich
   tomorrow.*

7. Sie trägt den Kindern den
   Koffer zum Bahnhof.
   *Sie tragen ihnen den Koffer
   zum Bahnhof.*

   She is taking the children's suitcase to
   the station.
   *She is taking the children's suitcase
   to the station.*

8. Sollen wir Herrn und Frau Müller
   in Berlin besuchen?
   *Sollen wir sie in Berlin
   besuchen?*

   Should we visit Mr and Mrs Mueller
   in Berlin?
   Should we visit them in Berlin?

9. Der Bahnangestellte gibt den
   Kunden die Fahrkarten.
   *Der Bahnangestellte gibt ihnen
   die Fahrkarten.*

   The travel agent is giving the customers
   their tickets.
   *The travel agent is giving them
   their tickets.*

10. Der Zug fährt Herrn Hammel
    nach Köln.
    Der Zug fährt ihn nach Köln.

    The train is taking Mr Hammel
    to Cologne.
    The train is taking him to Cologne.

Grammatik / Grammar

Der Dativ / The dative case

The use of the dative case is also determined by the verb. Some verbs always take the dative (helfen, schenken etc.)

With the dative case the articles in front of the nouns and the pronouns are changed.

> Ich helfe **dem** Mann.   Ich helfe **der** Frau.   Ich helfe **dem** Kind.

> Ich helfe **ihm**.   Ich helfe **ihr**.   Ich helfe **ihm**.

Vorsicht / Attention:
As you can see from the examples, feminine nouns can also take the definite article "**der**". Do not be confused by this – the noun gender remains feminine.

Entscheidungsfragen und W-Fragen / Yes-no and wh-questions.
Yes-no questions are always answered with "ja" or "nein". The most important indicator of a yes-no question is: the verb comes always at the beginning of the sentence. (this is one of the few exceptions to the rule that states that the verb comes second in a sentence.)

Die wh-questions however begin always with interrogatives:

Nominative	*"wer"* or *"was"*
Dative	*"wem"*
Accusative	*"wen"* or *"was"*
Temporal	*"wann"*
Locative	*"wo"*, *"wohin"*, *"worauf"*
Causative	*"warum"*
Modal	*"wie"*

Additional interrogative pronouns can be found in other lessons.

Entscheidungsfragen / Yes-no questions:

Gehst du morgen früh zum Bahnhof?
Are you going to the train station tomorrow morning?

Ja. (Ja, ich gehe zum Bahnhof).
(Yes, I am.)

Kommst du mich morgen Abend besuchen?
Are you going to visit me tomorrow evening.

Nein. (Nein, ich komme dich nicht besuchen.)
(No, I'm not.)

W-Fragen / Wh-questions:

Wer hat die Fahrkarten?
(Who has the tickets?

Andreas.
Andreas.)

Wem hilft der Kontrolleur?
(Who is the conductor helping?

Der alten Dame.
The old woman.)

Wen fragt der Fahrgast?
(Who is the passenger asking?

Den Kontrolleur.
The conductor.)

Wann kommt der Zug?
(When does the train arrive?

Um 11:00 Uhr.
At 11:00.)

Wohin fährt dieser Zug?
(Where does the train go to?

Nach Wuppertal.
To Wuppertal.)

Wo fährt der Zug nach Köln ab?
(Where does the train to Cologne depart?

Auf Bahnsteig 6.
Platform 6.)

Warum kommst du nicht?
(Why can't you come?

Wegen meiner Krankheit.
Because of my illness.)

Wie ist das Wetter in München?
(How is the weather in Munich?

Regnerisch.
Rainy.)

Präpositionen / Prepositions

In German you must distinguish between three groups of prepositions:

    a) Prepositions that take dative
    b) Prepositions that take accusative
    c) Prepositions that take either dative or accusative

a) The most important prepositions that take dative include: *"mit"*, *"von"*, *"zu"* and *"nach"*. You must always use the dative case with these prepositions.

> Ich fahre **mit der** Frau (**ihr**) nach München.
> *(I'm driving with the lady to Munich.)*
>
> Ich komme **von meiner** Arbeit nach Hause.
> *(I'm coming home from work.)*
>
> Ich gehe **zu dem** Kollegen (**ihm**).
> *(I am going to my colleague.)*

Because there is no article following **"nach"**, the dative case is often not recognisable.

b) The most important prepositions that take accusative are: *"für"*, *"gegen"*, *"bis"*, *"um"*

> Das Paket ist **für den** Mann (**ihn**).
> *(The package is for the man.)*
>
> Das Auto fährt **gegen den** Baum (**ihn**).
> *(The car hits the tree.)*
>
> Der Zug fährt **bis** München.
> *(The train goes to Munich.)*
>
> Er geht **um das** Haus (**es**).
> *(He goes around the house.)*

There is usually no article following the preposition **"bis"**.

c) The most important prepositions that take either dative or accusative (the so-called "doubtful" prepositions) are **"an"**, **"auf"**, **"hinter"**, **"in"**, **"neben"**, **"über"**, **"unter"**, **"vor"**

The case of the nouns after a "doubtful" preposition depends on the use of the preposition. When you are describing a goal of motion, you use the accusative after the preposition. The interrogative pronoun is **"wohin?"**.
If you are not describing a goal of motion, you use the dative case after the preposition. The interrogative pronoun is **"wo?"**.

Mishiko steht **auf dem** Bahnsteig.
(Mishiko is standing on the platform.)

Wo steht Mishiko?
(Where is Mishiko standing?)

Auf dem Bahnsteig.
(On the platform)

Mishiko geht **auf den** Bahnsteig.
(Mishiko is going to the platform)

Wohin geht Mishiko?
(Where is Mishiko going to?)

Auf den Bahnsteig.
(To the platform)

Hinweise / Important:

Die Uhrzeiten / The times of day

In German there is a big difference between the written and spoken forms of time. Even though the age of digital clocks has created its own language rules, situations where the written form is more applicable will take the following:

written:	**8:50 Uhr**
spoken:	**zehn vor neun**

written:	**20:50 Uhr**
spoken:	**zehn vor neun**

As you can see, written German uses the time system from 0:00 until 24:00; in spoken German the 12-hour system is used. (only in the form **zwanzig Uhr fünfzig** is the 24-hour system used.)

Bahnhof und Bahnfahrten / The train station and train travel

Tickets for the German rail are available in the larger train stations and in some travel agencies.
Because the network in German is very extensive and the trains are very frequent and punctual, travel by train is very confortable.

The designations for the long-distance trains are:
- ICE   Intercity Express
- EC   Eurocity
- IC   Intercity
- IR   Interregio

The **ICE** trains are the fastest trains in Germany. They only stop in the larger cities. These trains require an additional surcharge, but the cost is not that much higher than a standard ticket.

You can also travel quickly with the **IC** and **EC** trains. If you want to take these trains, there is also an additional surcharge.

The **IR** also runs long distances. But because it stops in smaller cities as well, this train is not as quick as the ICE and the IC/EC.

When you buy your ticket at the ticket counter, you will receive a detailed travel plan for your journey. There you will find all important departure times and train stations where you have to change trains.
Here you also have the possibility to reserve a seat. Because these seat reservations only cost a little more than a standard ticket, a reserved seat is recommended for many trains. Otherwise you may find that you must spend a portion of your trip standing (you should also indicate whether you desire a seat in the smoking or non-smoking sections).

If you have missed the opportunity to buy your ticket in advance, you may have the chance to buy your ticket from the conductor. You should, however, contact the conductor as soon as possible, so that you are not suspected of "Schwarzfahren" or trying to ride for free.

Schriftliche Übungen / Written exercises

Insert the correct article in the nominative, dative, or accusative case.

a) _____ Zug fährt um 6:11 nach Wuppertal.

b) _____ Kontrolleur gibt _____ Fahrgast _____ Fahrschein.

c) Herr Meier reist mit _____ Familie nach München.

d) _____ Zug hält auf _____ Bahnsteig 6.

e) Dorothee geht heute nicht in _____ Schule.

f) Sie fahren mit _____ Zug von Wuppertal nach München.

g) _____ Angestellte gibt _____ Kunden (Singular) _____ die Fahrkarte für _____ Raucherabteil.

h) _____ ICE ist schneller als _____ IC.

i) _____ Mutter setzt sich auf _____ Stuhl.

j) _____ Vater sitzt auf _____ Sessel.

k) _____ neue Bild hängt an _____ Wand.

l) _____ Auto steht neben _____ Bahnhof.

Ask questions about the underlined information in each sentence.

a) Der Zug erreicht München um 18:00 Uhr.

b) Andreas fährt das Auto in die Garage.

c) Der Bahnhof liegt im Stadtzentrum.

d) Der Kunde kauft eine Fahrkarte nach Köln.

e) Wolfgang fährt in die Stadt.

f) Mishiko ist das zweite Mal in Deutschland.

g) Der Bahnhof liegt zwischen dem Hotel und der Bank.

h) Die Kinder schenken den Eltern zu Weihnachten ein Buch.

i) Mishiko kann heute nicht zur Arbeit gehen.

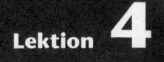

Lektion 4

Telefonieren

CD2
TOP1 Telephoning in a foreign language is an uncomfortable situation for many people. Because you cannot see your telephone partner, you cannot interpret body language and gestures to help understand the message.
In the following lesson you can listen to and see the most important instructions for telephoning in Germany.

You will learn:

- How you should answer and receive calls;
- How to say goodbye;
- How to use a public phone;

Wichtige Formulierungen! / Important phrases:
First, listen to these phrases:

Wählen Sie die Nummer 123456.	Please dial the number 123456.
Ich möchte gerne einen Termin vereinbaren.	I would like to make an appointment.
Können Sie bitte Ihren Namen buchstabieren?	Could you spell your name, please?
Ich werde Ihre Nachricht weiterleiten.	I will pass on your message.
Kann ich Ihnen helfen?	Can I help you?
Hier spricht Lothar Seuthe von der Firma Teleport.	This is Lothar Seuthe from Teleport.
Ich hätte gern die Nummer eines Teilnehmers in München.	I would like the number of a participant in Munich.
Rufen Sie doch die Auskunft an!	Please call information.
Ich werde gleich zurückrufen.	I will call you right back.
Auf Wiederhören.	Good bye.

CD2 Dialogue
TOP2

Now listen to the following dialogue:

Mishiko wants to contact a German firm in Munich. Her Japanese company is interested in having closer ties between the two firms. Mishiko is calling Munich to set an appointment with her German colleagues. She calls the central office and speaks first with a telphone operator.

Mishiko:
Guten Tag. Hier ist Mishiko Thai.

Mishiko:
Hello, this is Mishiko Thai.

Telefonistin:
Kann ich Ihnen helfen?

telphone operator:
Can I help you?

Mishiko:
Könnte ich bitte Herrn Seuthe sprechen?

Mishiko:
Could I speak to Mr. Seuthe, please?

Telefonistin:
Es tut mir Leid, aber Herr Seuthe spricht gerade. Ich gebe Ihnen am besten seine Durchwahl. Wählen Sie bitte die 123456!

telphone operator:
I'm sorry, but Mr. Seuthe is on another line. Let me give you his extension. It's 123456!

Mishiko:
Danke.

Mishiko:
Thank you.

Telefonistin:
Oh, ich sehe, dass Herr Seuthe nun frei ist. Ich verbinde Sie.

telphone operator:
Oh, now Mr. Seuthe is free. I will put you through.

Herr Seuthe:
Seuthe.

Mr. Seuthe
Hello, Seuthe here.

Mishiko:
Guten Tag Herr Seuthe. Hier spricht Frau Thai von der Firma Cason.

Mishiko:
Hello Mr. Seuthe, this is Miss Thai from the Cason company.

Herr Seuthe:
Ja, Guten Tag Frau Thai. Sind Sie gut in Deutschland angekommen?

Mr. Seuthe
Hello Miss Thai. Did you have a pleasant journey to Germany?

Mishiko:
Ja, danke. Ich hatte eine gute Reise.

Mishiko:
Yes, thank you, it was fine.

Herr Seuthe:
Wo sind sie denn zur Zeit?
Befinden Sie sich schon in München?

Mr. Seuthe
Where are you calling from?
Are you in Munich?

Mishiko:
Nein, ich bin noch in Köln. Ich komme
aber morgen nach München. Können
Sie mir dort ein Hotel empfehlen?

Mishiko:
No, I'm still in Cologne, but I'm travelling
to Munich tomorrow. Can you recommend
a good hotel?

Herr Seuthe:
Ich empfehle Ihnen das Hotel Rose. Es
ist wirklich sehr schön. Leider weiß ich
die Telefonnummer nicht. Am besten
rufen Sie die Auskunft an und lassen
sich die Nummer geben.

Mr. Seuthe
I recommend the Hotel Rose. It's very nice.
Unfortunately, I don't know the phone number.
Your best bet would be to call information
to get the number.

Mishiko:
Wie war der Name des Hotels? Ich
habe es nicht richtig verstanden.

Mishiko:
What was the name of the hotel? I didn't
catch the name.

Herr Seuthe:
Hotel Rose.

Mr. Seuthe
Hotel Rose.

Mishiko:
Können Sie den Namen bitte
buchstabieren?

Mishiko:
Could you please spell that for me?

Herr Seuthe:
R-O-S-E.

Mr. Seuthe
R-O-S-E.

Mishiko:
Danke. Ich komme gegen 17:00 Uhr
dort an.

Mishiko:
Thank you. I'm arriving in Munich at around
5 p.m.

Herr Seuthe:
Schön. Aber jetzt sollten wir zum
Geschäftlichen kommen. Vielleicht
sollten wir zuerst einen Termin
vereinbaren. Wann würde es Ihnen
denn am besten passen?

Mr. Seuthe
Great. Now we need to discuss some business.
Perhaps we should make an appointment.
When would be best for you?

Mishiko:
Wie wäre es mit übermorgen
um 10:30 Uhr?

Mishiko:
How about the day after tomorrow
at 10:30 a.m.?

Herr Seuthe:
Das passt mir gut. Kommen
Sie zu mir ins Büro?

Mr. Seuthe
That suits me fine. Do you want to come
to my office?

Mishiko:
Ja.

Mishiko:
Yes.

Herr Seuthe:
Gut, dann erwarte ich Sie um
10:30 Uhr in meinem Büro. Wissen
Sie, wo unsere Firma ist? Ich schlage
vor, dass Sie mich vom Bahnhof aus
anrufen, dann werde ich Sie dort abholen.

Mr. Seuthe
Good, then I'll be expecting you at 10:30 in
my office. Do you know where we are located?
I suggest that you call me from the train
station, then I'll come by and pick you up.

Mishiko:
Das ist sehr liebenswürdig von Ihnen.
Dann bis übermorgen. Auf Wiederhören.

Mishiko:
That's very nice of you.
So, until then, goodbye.

Herr Seuthe:
Bis übermorgen. Auf Wiederhören.

Mr. Seuthe
Until then. Goodbye.

**Mishiko ruft nun die Auskunft an, um die Telefonnummer des Hotels in
München zu bekommen.**
*Now, Mishiko is calling information to get the phone number of the hotel in
Munich.*

Mishiko:
Guten Tag, ich hätte gern die Nummer
eines Teilnehmers in München.

Mishiko:
Hello. I would like to know the number of
a business in Munich.

Auskunft:
Ja, wie lautet der Name des Teilnehmers?

Operator:
Ok, what is the name of the business?

Mishiko:
Hotel Rose.

Mishiko:
The Hotel Rose.

Auskunft:
Augenblick. Die gewünschte
Nummer wird nun angesagt.

Operator:
One moment, please. You will now hear
the number you want.

Bandansage:
Die Nummer lautet: 4-5-6-7-8-9.
Die Vorwahl lautet 0-8-9.

Recorded message:
The number is: 4-5-6-7-8-9.
The city code is 0-8-9.

I recommend that you listen to the entire dialogue one more time. You should also repeat the individual sentences so that you can get the right feeling for the correct pronunciation.
(If the dialogue is too fast, please use the pause button on your CD player.)

CD2 TOP3 Übung 1 / Exercise 1:

In this exercise you will learn the second very important verb form in the German language: **the present perfect tense.**
As you already know, you can use the present tense for all situations that occur in the present or will occur in the future.
In German, you can use the present perfect for everything that happened in the past. It makes absolutely no difference whether something happened a few minutes ago or many years in the past.
Please keep in mind that the present perfect is used with the auxiliory verbs "**sein**" und "**haben**". Additional information on this subject can be found in the grammar section.

Now, transform these present-tense sentences into present perfect:

B Beispiel / Example:

Sprecher:	*Mishiko ist in Deutschland.*
Speaker:	*Mishiko is in Germany.*
Sie:	*Mishiko ist in Deutschland gewesen.*
You:	*Mishiko was in Germany.*
Sprecher:	*Andreas hat keine Zeit.*
Speaker:	*Andreas has no time.*
Sie:	*Andreas hat keine Zeit gehabt.*
You:	*Andreas had no time.*
Sprecher:	*Herrn Seuthes Büro liegt in München.*
Speaker:	*Mr. Seuthe's office is in Munich.*
Sie:	*Herrn Seuthes Büro hat in München gelegen.*
You:	*Mr. Seuthe's office was in Munich.*
Sprecher:	*Andreas fährt zu seinem Büro in Köln.*
Speaker:	*Andreas is driving to his office in Cologne.*
Sie:	*Andreas ist zu seinem Büro in Köln gefahren.*
You:	*Andreas drove to his office in Cologne.*

1.
2.
3.

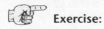 **Exercise:**

1. Mishiko ist in Deutschland.   Mishiko is in Germany.
   Mishiko ist in Deutschland gewesen.   *Mishiko was in Germany.*

2. Andreas hat keine Zeit.   Andreas has no time.
   Andreas hat keine Zeit gehabt.   *Andreas had no time.*

3. Herrn Seuthes Büro liegt in München.   Mr. Seuthe's office is in Munich.
   Herrn Seuthes Büro hat in   *Mr. Seuthe's office was in*
   München gelegen.   *Munich.*

4. Andreas fährt zu seinem Büro in Köln.   Andreas is driving to his office in Cologne.
   Andreas ist zu seinem Büro   *Andreas drove to his office in Cologne.*
   in Köln gefahren.

5. Mishiko spricht mit Herrn   Mishiko is speaking to Mr. Seuthe about
   Seuthe über die Zusammenarbeit   the two companies' working together.
   der beiden Unternehmen.
   Mishiko hat mit Herrn Seuthe   *Mishiko spoke to Mr. Seuthe about*
   über die Zusammenarbeit der   *the two companies' working together.*
   beiden Unternehmen gesprochen.

6. Mishiko ruft die Auskunft   Mishiko is calling information to find
   wegen einer Telefonnummer   a phone number in Munich.
   in München an.
   Mishiko hat die Auskunft   *Mishiko called information to find*
   wegen einer Telefonnummer   *a phone number in Munich.*
   in München angerufen.

7. Der Kontrolleur überprüft die   The conductor is checking the
   Fahrkarten der Reisenden.   passengers' tickets.
   Der Kontrolleur hat die Fahrkarten   *The conductor checked the passengers'*
   der Reisenden überprüft.   *tickets.*

8. Herr Lehmann kann leider   Unfortunately, Mr. Lehmann cannot be
   nicht an dem Empfang teilnehmen.   at the reception.
   Herr Lehmann hat leider an dem   *Unfortunately, Mr. Lehmann could*
   Empfang nicht teilnehmen können.   *not be at the reception.*

9. Der ICE erreicht pünktlich
   den Wuppertaler Hauptbahnhof.
   Der ICE hat den Wuppertaler
   Hauptbahnhof pünktlich erreicht.

   The ICE is arriving at Wuppertal train
   station on time.
   The ICE arrived at Wuppertal train
   station on time.

10. Die Verabredung zwischen
    Mishiko und Herrn Seuthe
    dauert 45 Minuten.
    Die Verabredung zwischen
    Mishiko und Herrn Seuthe
    hat 45 Minuten gedauert.

    The conversation between Mishiko and
    Mr. Seuthe lasts 45 minutes.

    The conversation between Mishiko
    and Mr. Seuthe lasted 45 minutes.

11. Sie kommen pünktlich
    in der Firma an.
    Sie sind pünktlich in der
    Firma angekommen.

    She is arriving at the company on time.

    She arrived at the company on time.

12. Du hast die Dokumente
    in deiner Tasche.
    Du hast die Dokumente in
    deiner Tasche gehabt.

    You have the documents in your pocket.

    You had the documents in your pocket.

13. Ihr wollt an dem Empfang
    im Hotel nicht teilnehmen.
    Ihr habt an dem Empfang im
    Hotel nicht teilnehmen wollen.

    You don't want to be at the reception.

    You didn't want to be at the reception.

**CD2
TOP4** # Übung 2 / Exercise 2:

In this exercise you will familiarise yourself with how to use the modal verbs.
You should learn the following modal verbs:

> Dürfen (may, be allowed), können (can, be able to), müssen (must, have to),
> sollen (should), wollen (want to).

 Beispiel / Example:

Sprecher: *Herr Lehmann nimmt die Medizin.*
Speaker: *Mr. Lehmann is taking the medicine.*

Sprecher: *Der Arzt hat es empfohlen.*
Speaker: *The doctor recommended it.*

Sie: *Herr Lehmann soll die Medizin nehmen.*
You: *Mr. Lehmann should take the medicine.*

Sprecher: *Mishiko ruft ihren Chef in Japan an.*
Speaker: *Mishiko is calling her boss in Japan.*

Sprecher: *Es ist sehr wichtig.*
Speaker: *It is very important.*

Sie: *Mishiko muss ihren Chef in Japan anrufen.*
You: *Mishiko has to call her boss in Japan.*

 **Exercise:**

1. Herr Lehmann nimmt die Medizin.
   Der Arzt hat es empfohlen.
   Herr Lehmann soll die Medizin nehmen.

   Mr. Lehmann is taking the medicine.
   The doctor recommended it.
   Mr. Lehmann should take the medicine.

2. Mishiko ruft ihren Chef in Japan an.
   Es ist sehr wichtig.
   Mishiko muss ihren Chef in Japan anrufen.

   Mishiko is calling her boss in Japan.
   It is very important.
   Mishiko has to call her boss in Japan.

3. Das Kind geht ins Kino.
   Es hat die Erlaubnis.
   Das Kind darf ins Kino gehen.

   The child is going to the cinema.
   It has permission.
   The child is allowed to go to the cinema.

4. Mishiko spricht Deutsch.
   Sie hat es gelernt.
   Mishiko kann Deutsch sprechen.

   Mishiko speaks German.
   She studied it.
   Mishiko can speak German.

5. Herr Seuthe reist nach Wuppertal.
   Er macht es sehr gern.
   Herr Seuthe will nach Wuppertal reisen.

   Mr. Seuthe is travelling to Wuppertal.
   He likes to do it.
   Mr. Seuthe wants to travel to Wuppertal

6. Mishiko geht morgen
   Nachmittag zum Arzt.
   Es ist sehr wichtig.
   Mishiko muss morgen Nachmittag zum Arzt gehen.

   Mishiko is going to the doctor
   tomorrow afternoon.
   It is very important.
   Mishiko has to go to the doctor tomorrow afternoon.

7. Andreas lädt Mishiko zum
   Essen in ein Restaurant ein.
   Er macht es sehr gern.
   Andreas will Mishiko zum Esssen in ein Restaurant einladen.

   Andreas is inviting Mishiko to dinner
   in a restaurant.
   He likes to do it.
   Andreas wants to invite Mishiko to dinner in a restaurant.

8. Herr Bryan lernt in einer
Schule Deutsch.
Sein Kollege hat es empfohlen.
***Herr Bryan soll in einer Schule
Deutsch lernen.***

Mr. Bryan is studying German at a
school.
His colleague recommended it.
***Mr. Bryan should study German
at a school.***

9. Mishiko nimmt heute
einen freien Tag.
Sie hat die Erlaubnis.
***Mishiko darf heute einen
freien Tag nehmen.***

Mishiko is taking a day off.

She has permission to do so.
***Mishiko is allowed to take a day
off today.***

10. Herr Lehmann spricht
drei Fremdsprachen.
Er hat es gelernt.
***Herr Lehmann kann drei
Fremdsprachen sprechen.***

Mr. Lehmann speaks three foreign
languages.
He learned it.
***Mr. Lehmann can speak three
foreign languages.***

Grammatik / Grammar

1. Das Perfekt / The present perfect

Next to the present tense, the present perfect is the second most important verb tense in the German language.
Everything that happened in the past can be described using the present perfect. To create the present perfect, you need an auxiliary verb (*"haben"* or *"sein"*) and the past participle of the main verb.

– You must distinguish between the *"weak"* and the *"strong"* verbs in German. (the strong verbs are the irregular verbs.) (See the verb list in the appendix.) With the past participle you will recognise the strong verbs by their ending -*en*; they also often have an umlaut; while the weak verbs are distinguished by the ending -t.
Both forms begin with *ge-* .

– In the most cases, the present perfect is formed with the auxiliary verb *"haben"*. However, if a sentence describes motion or the beginning or end of a process, you must use *"sein"* as the auxiliary verb.

– The auxiliary verb always comes second in a sentence, and the past participle always comes at the end of the sentence.

Present perfect with weak verbs:

Er reist nach Köln.   Er ist nach Köln gereist.
(He is travelling to Cologne. He travelled to Cologne.)

Er macht seine Arbeit.   Er hat seine Arbeit gemacht.
(He does his work.   He did his work.)

Present perfect with strong verbs:

Er geht ins Büro.   Er ist ins Büro gegangen.
(He is going to his office. He went to his office.)

Er spricht mit seinem Chef. Er hat mit seinem Chef gesprochen.
(He is speaking with his boss. He spoke with his boss.)

2. Präteritum von *"haben"* und *"sein"*
   Present perfect with *"haben"* (to have) and *"sein"* (to be):

Even though you can express everything in the past with the present perfect, sentences with the main verbs "haben" or "sein" are mostly expressed in the simple past tense. If you write in German, however, the present perfect is most often used in these cases.

The simple past of these verbs is:

haben	hatte
sein	war

Conjugation:

ich	hatte	war
du	hattest	warst
er	hatte	war
sie	hatte	war
es	hatte	war
wir	hatten	waren
ihr	hattet	wart
sie/Sie	hatten	waren

Er ist in Köln.	Er war in Köln.
(He is in Cologne.	*He was in Cologne.)*
Er hat keine Zeit.	Er hatte keine Zeit.
(He has no time.	*He had no time.)*

3. Modalverben / Modal verbs

When you use the German modal verbs

dürfen, können, möchten, müssen, sollen, wollen

you must always make sure that the correctly conjugated modal verb comes second in the sentence. The main verb (in the infinitive form) always is at the end of the sentence.

> Er spricht mit seinem Kollegen.
> *(He speaks with his colleague)*

> Er muss mit seinem Kollegen sprechen.
> *(He must speak with his colleague)*

Hinweise / Important:

Verhaltensweisen am Telefon /
Proper telephone manners:
In Germany it is normal to announce your name when you make phone calls, regardless if you are making or receiving the call. A conversation that only begins with a simple *"Hallo"* is considered very impolite.
This rule is true both for private and business phone calls.
For business calls, you can also include the name of your employer after you announce your name.
At the end of the phone call, you normally use the phrase *"Auf Wiederhören"* (until I hear from you again). *"Auf Wiedersehen"* (until I see you again) is not appropriate because you cannot actually see your conversation partner.

Telefonieren von öffentlichen Fernsprechzellen /
Telephoning from public phones
There are many public phones in Germany. You will never have a problem locating one.
In recent years, almost all pay phones are now operated with phone cards, making it necessary to buy a telephone card.
You can find these telephone cards at the German post office, as well as in many retail stores. (These stores will have signs indicating that they sell phone cards.)
For most long-distance calls you can also use credit cards.

Schriftliche Übungen / Written exercises

Please insert the correct form of *"haben"* or *"sein"*:

a) Andreas _____ gestern Abend in Köln angekommen.

b) Mishiko _____ nach ihrer Ankunft in Deutschland sofort ihren Chef in Tokio angerufen.

c) Die Kollegen _____ sich über den Anruf gefreut.

d) Du _____ schon wieder zu spät zur Arbeit gekommen.

e) Ihr _____ vergessen, die Karten für die Zugfahrt zu reservieren.

f) Andreas und Mishiko _____ sich heute Abend in München verabredet.

g) Wir _____ im letzten Jahr zusammen mit Freunden nach Japan gefahren.

h) Es _____ heute schon wieder den ganzen Tag geregnet.

i) Ich _____ die ganze Woche zu Fuß zur Arbeit gegangen.

j) Du _____ hast vergessen, die Fenster in deinem Büro zu schließen.

Please insert the correct verb endings:

a) Herr Seuthe und Herr Lehmann sind am Mittwoch nach Berlin gereis_____.

b) Du hast nicht an die Reisepässe gedach_____.

c) Wir haben letzte Woche sehr gut in einem neuen Restaurant gegess_____.

d) Ich habe meinen Freunden eine Karte aus Japan geschrieb_____.

e) Die Kollegen haben an einer wichtigen Besprechung teilgenomm_____.

f) Herr Lehmann hat mir nicht geglaub_____.

g) Wir haben für heute Abend einen sehr guten Wein gekauf_____.

h) Mishiko hat mit ihrem Chef gesproch_____.

i) Andreas hat das Telefongespräch nach einer halben Stunde beende_____.

j) Ich habe meine Brieftasche im Hotel liegengelass_____.

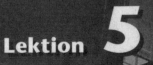

Essen und Trinken gehen

CD2
TOP5 There are not many differences between visiting restaurants in different countries. However, it is important to know how to behave in such situations here in Germany. In this lesson you will of course learn the most important expressions for visits to restaurants and to read a menu.

Wichtige Formulierungen! / Important phrases!

Listen first to these phrases:

Ich möchte gern einen Platz für drei Personen reservieren.
I would like to reserve a table for three, please.

Wir möchten um 19:00 Uhr kommen.
We would like to come at 7 p.m.

Ist der Fensterplatz dort noch frei?
Is there a table with a view available?

Darf ich Ihnen schon etwas zu trinken bringen?
Can I get you something to drink?

Wir hätten gern die Speisekarte.
We would like the menu, please.

Als Vorspeise hätte ich gern eine Suppe.
As a starter, I will take the soup, please.

Bringen Sie jetzt bitte das Hauptgericht.
Please bring us the main course now.

Welchen Nachtisch würden Sie mir empfehlen?
What would you recommend for dessert?

Ich möchte einen trockenen Rotwein.
I would like a dry red wine, please.

Darf ich Ihnen noch ein Glas Bier bringen?
Can I offer you another glass of beer?

Bedienung, bringen Sie mir bitte die Rechnung.
Waiter, could you bring us the check, please.

Kann ich auch mit meiner Kreditkarte zahlen?
Can I pay with a credit card?

Guten Appetit.
Bon appetite!

Dialog 5 / Dialogue 5

Now listen to the following dialogue:

Mishiko, Andreas and Mr. Seuthe would like to go out for dinner tonight. Andreas is calling up a restaurant to reserve a table.

Andreas: Guten Tag. Hier ist Peters. Ich möchte gerne einen Platz für drei Personen reservieren.	*Andreas:* Hello, this is Mr. Peters. I would like to reserve a table for three.
Kellnerin: Um wie viel Uhr möchten Sie denn kommen, Herr Peters?	*Waitress:* And for what time, Mr. Peters?
Andreas: Wir möchten heute Abend um 19:00 Uhr kommen. Haben Sie da noch einen Tisch frei?	*Andreas:* We would like a table tonight for 7 p.m. Do you have a table available for that time?
Kellnerin: Ja, ich werde ihn auf Ihren Namen reservieren.	*Waitress:* Yes, we do. I'll reserve it under your name.
Andreas: Danke. Auf Wiederhören.	*Andreas:* Thank you. Good bye.
Kellnerin: Auf Wiederhören.	*Waitress:* Good bye.

Mishiko, Andreas and Mr. Seuthe are entering a restaurant and the hostess greets them.

Kellnerin: Was kann ich für Sie tun?	*Waitress:* Hello. What can I do for you?
Andreas: Ich hatte einen Tisch auf den Namen Peters reserviert.	*Andreas:* I have a table reserved under the name Peters.
Kellnerin: Ja, Herr Peters. Gefällt Ihnen dieser Platz dort?	*Waitress:* Oh yes, Mr. Peters. Is this table ok?

Andreas:
Ist dieser Fensterplatz dort noch frei?

Andreas:
Is this place next to the window still available?

Kellnerin:
Nein, leider nicht. Dieser Tisch
ist reserviert.

Waitress:
No, unfortunately not. This table is
already reserved.

Andreas:
Schade. Dann nehmen wir diesen Tisch.

Andreas:
Too bad. Then, we will take this table instead.

Kellnerin:
Darf ich Ihnen schon etwas
zu trinken bringen?

Waitress:
Can I get you something to drink?

Andreas:
Wir hätte gern zuerst die Speisekarte.
(zu den Anderen)
Was möchten Sie denn trinken?

Andreas:
We would like to see the menus first.
(to the others)
What would you like to drink?

Mishiko:
Ich möchte gern einen trockenen Rotwein.

Mishiko:
I would like a glass of dry red wine please.

Herr Seuthe:
Ich trinke ein Glas Bier.

Mr. Seuthe:
A glass of beer, please.

Kellnerin:
So, hier sind die Speisekarten.

Waitress:
Here are your menus.

Andreas:
Bringen Sie uns bitte einen trockenen
Rotwein und zwei Gläser Pils.

Andreas:
Please could you bring us a glass of dry
red wine and two glasses of beer?

Kellnerin:
Gerne.

Waitress:
Certainly.

Andreas:
Weißt du schon, was du als
Vorspeise nimmst?

Andreas:
Do you already know what you want for
a starter?

Mishiko:
Als Vorspeise hätte ich gern
eine Tomatensuppe.

Mishiko:
For starters, I will have a bowl of tomato
soup, please.

Herr Seuthe:
Ich nehme eine Pastete.

Mr. Seuthe:
I'll take a vol-a-vent, please.

Andreas:
Ich nehme das Pilzomelett.

Andreas:
I'll have the mushroom omelette, please.

Kellnerin:	*Waitress:*
Möchten Sie auch schon die anderen Gänge bestellen?	Would you also like to order your main course now?
Andreas:	*Andreas:*
Für mich bitte „Rheinischer Sauerbraten".	I'll take the Rheinland Sauerbraten.
Mishiko:	*Mishiko:*
Was ist denn Sauerbraten?	What exactly is Sauerbraten?
Kellnerin:	*Waitress:*
Das ist Rindfleisch, das in einer Marinade eingelegt wurde.	It is beef marinated in a special sauce.
Mishiko:	*Mishiko:*
Oh, das möchte ich probieren.	Oh, that sounds good. I'll try that.
Herr Seuthe:	*Mr. Seuthe:*
Bringen Sie mir bitte einmal Hirschgulasch mit Klößen.	And I'll have the venison with dumplings, please.
Kellnerin:	*Waitress:*
Danke für die Bestellung.	Thank you for your order.
Herr Seuthe:	*Mr. Seuthe:*
Guten Appetit zusammen.	Bon appetite, everyone
Andreas:	*Andreas:*
Jetzt habe ich Durst. Zum Wohl.	Now, I'm thirsty. To your health.
Mishiko:	*Mishiko:*
Zum Wohl.	To your health.
Herr Seuthe:	*Mr. Seuthe:*
Prost.	Cheers!
Mishiko:	*Mishiko:*
Das Essen war sehr gut.	The food was very good indeed.
Andreas:	*Andreas:*
Was sollen wir denn zum Nachtisch nehmen?	What should we order for dessert?
Herr Seuthe:	*Mr. Seuthe:*
Ich glaube, ich nehme ein Eis.	I think I'll have the ice cream.
Andreas:	*Andreas:*
Das ist eine gute Idee. Mishiko, möchtest du auch ein Eis als Nachtisch?	That sounds good. Mishiko, would you also like ice cream for dessert?

Mishiko:
Nein danke. Ich habe genug gegessen.

Mishiko:
No thanks, I've had enough already.

Andreas:
Herr Ober, bringen Sie uns bitte
noch zwei Portionen Eis.

Andreas:
Excuse me, waiter, could you bring us
two portions of ice cream?

Kellnerin:
Sofort.

Waitress:
Right away, sir.

Herr Seuthe:
Bedienung, würden Sie mir bitte jetzt
die Rechnung bringen.

Mr. Seuthe:
Madame, could you bring me the
check, please?

Kellnerin:
Die Rechnung, mein Herr.

Waitress:
Here is your check, sir.

Herr Seuthe:
Kann ich auch mit meiner
Kreditkarte bezahlen?

Mr. Seuthe:
Can I also pay with a credit card?

Kellnerin:
Selbstverständlich.

Waitress:
Certainly.

Andreas:
Das war wirklich sehr gut. Schönen
Dank für Ihre Einladung.

Andreas:
That was really good. Thank you for
your invitation.

Mishiko:
Ich möchte mich auch bedanken.
Das war sehr nett, dass sie
uns eingeladen haben.

Mishiko:
I also have to thank you. That was
very nice of you to invite us

Herr Seuthe:
Gern geschehen. Es war mir ein Vergnügen.

Mr. Seuthe:
Glad to do it. It was my pleasure.

D2 I recommend that you listen to the whole dialogue a second time. You should
OP7 now repeat the individual sentences, so that you can get a feeling for the
correct responses.
(If the dialogue is too fast, please use the pause button on your
CD player.)

Übung 1 / Exercise 1:

 Beispiel / Example:

Sprecher:	*Die Kellnerin bringt den Teller.*
	Der Teller ist sehr heiß.
Speaker:	*The waitress brings the plates.*
	The plate is very hot.
Sie:	*Die Kellnerin bringt den heißen Teller.*
You:	*The waitress brings the hot plate.*
Sprecher:	*Er trinkt das Bier.*
	Das Bier ist kalt.
Speaker:	*He drinks the beer.*
	The beer is cold.
Sie:	*Er trinkt das kalte Bier.*
You:	*He drinks the cold beer.*
Sprecher:	*Mishiko isst Sauerbraten.*
	Der Sauerbraten ist gut.
Speaker:	*Mishiko eats Sauerbraten.*
	The Sauerbraten is good.
Sie:	*Mishiko isst den guten Sauerbraten.*
You:	*Mishiko eats the good Sauerbraten.*

Übung 2 / Exercise 2

In German, when you use nouns that have not been used in earlier sentences, you should use the indefinite article. Only after the introduction of a noun should you use the definite article.
The indefinite article only has a plural form in negative sentences.

B **Beispiel / Example:**

Sprecher:	*Dort stehen vier Autos.*
Speaker:	*There are four cars over there.*
Sie:	*Dort stehen keine Autos.*
You:	*There are no cars over there.*
Sprecher:	*Morgen kommen mich meine zwei Freunde besuchen.*
Speaker:	*Tomorrow my two friends are coming to visit me.*
Sie:	*Morgen kommen mich keine Freunde besuchen.*
You:	*Tomorrow no one is coming to visit me.*

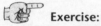 **Exercise:**

1. Dort stehen vier Autos.
   Dort stehen keine Autos.

   There are four cars over there.
   There are no cars over there.

2. Morgen kommen mich meine zwei Freunde besuchen.
   Morgen kommen mich keine Freunde besuchen.

   Tomorrow my two friends are coming to visit me.
   Tomorrow no one is coming to visit me.

3. 25 Gäste sind in dem Restaurant.
   In dem Restaurant sind keine Gäste.

   There are 25 guests in the restaurant.
   There are no guests in the restaurant.

4. Der Mann hat 15 Katzen zu Hause.
   Der Mann hat keine Katzen zu Hause.

   The man has 15 cats in his house.
   The man has no cats in his house.

5. Auf der Fahrt nach München muss Mishiko dreimal umsteigen.
   Auf der Fahrt nach München muss Mishiko keinmal umsteigen.

   On the trip to Munich Mishiko must change trains three times.
   On the trip to Munich Mishiko doesn't have to change trains.

6. Seine beiden Kinder warten
   in der Stadt auf ihn.
   In der Stadt warten keine
   Kinder auf ihn.

   Both of his children are waiting for
   him in the city.
   No children are waiting for him
   in the city.

7. Andreas hat der Kellnerin
   viel Trinkgeld gegeben.
   Andreas hat der Kellnerin
   kein Trinkgeld gegeben.

   Andreas gave the waitress a big tip.

   Andreas didn't give the waitress a tip.

8. Der Autofahrer muss 40 DM
   Strafe bezahlen.
   Der Autofahrer muss keine
   Strafe bezahlen.

   The driver has to pay a 40 DM fine.

   The driver doesn't have to pay a fine.

9. Die Kellnerin bringt den
   Gästen die Speisekarte.
   Die Kellnerin bringt den Gästen
   keine Speisekarte.

   The waitress is bringing the guests
   a menu.
   The waitress isn't bringing the
   guests a menu.

Übung 3 / Exercise 3

As you just have heard, you use the article "kein" (no) to negate nouns.
When you wish to negate a verb, you must use "nicht" (not).

B Beispiel / Example:

Sprecher: *Andreas hat heute viel Zeit.*
Speaker: *Andreas has a lot of time today.*

Sie: *Andreas hat heute keine Zeit.*
You: *Andreas has no time today.*

Sprecher: *Mishiko soll heute kommen.*
Speaker: *Mishiko should come today.*

Sie: *Mishiko soll heute nicht kommen.*
You: *Mishiko should not come today.*

Exercise:

1. Mishiko bestellt einen Nachtisch.   Mishiko is ordering a dessert.
   Mishiko bestellt keinen Nachtisch.   *Mishiko is ordering no dessert.*

2. Die Kellnerin hat die Getränke   The waitress brought the drinks.
   gebracht.
   Die Kellnerin hat keine Getränke   *The waitress brought no drinks.*
   gebracht.

3. Herr Seuthe ist sehr schnell nach   Mr. Seuthe drove to Munich
   München gefahren.   very quickly.
   Herr Seuthe ist nicht sehr schnell   *Mr. Seuthe didn't drive to*
   nach München gefahren.   *Munich very quickly.*

4. Sie wollen mit der Firma einen   They want to sign a contract with
   Vertrag schließen.   the company.
   Sie wollen mit der Firma keinen   *They want to sign no contract*
   Vertrag schließen.   *with the company.*

5. Andreas und Mishiko sitzen im   Andreas and Mishiko are sitting in
   Restaurant.   the restaurant.
   Andreas und Mishiko sitzen nicht   *Andreas and Mishiko are not sitting*
   im Restaurant.   *in the restaurant.*

6. Er fährt mit dem Auto zur Arbeit.   He is driving to work in his car.
   Er fährt nicht mit dem Auto   *He isn't driving to work in his car.*
   zur Arbeit.

7. Herr Seuthe hat im Restaurant ein   Mr. Seuthe drank a beer in the
   Bier getrunken.   restaurant.
   Herr Seuthe hat im Restaurant   *Mr. Seuthe drank no beer in*
   kein Bier getrunken.   *the restaurant.*

8. Mishiko will morgen Abend in   Mishiko wants to call Tokyo
   Tokio anrufen.   tomorrow evening.
   Mishiko will morgen Abend nicht   *Mishiko doesn't want to call*
   in Tokio anrufen.   *Tokyo tomorrow evening.*

9. Sie können in diesem Restaurant mit ihrer Kreditkarte bezahlen.
Sie können in diesem Restaurant nicht mit ihrer Kreditkarte bezahlen.

They can pay with a credit card in this restaurant.
They can't pay with a credit card in this restaurant.

10. Herr Lehmann unterschreibt den Vertrag.
Herr Lehmann unterschreibt keinen Vertrag.

Mr. Lehmann signs the contract.
Mr. Lehmann signs no contract.

11. Herr Lehmann will den Vertrag unterschreiben.
Herr Lehmann will den Vertrag nicht unterschreiben.

Mr. Lehmann wants to sign the contract.
Mr. Lehmann doesn't want to sign the contract.

12. Mishiko nimmt die Tabletten.
Mishiko nimmt keine Tabletten.

Mishiko is taking the tablets.
Mishiko is taking no tablets.

13. Mishiko muss die Tabletten nehmen.
Mishiko muss die Tabletten nicht nehmen.

Mishiko has to take the tablets.

Mishiko doesn't have to take the tablets.

Grammatik / Grammar

Die Adjektivdeklination / The declination of adjectives

You have two possible ways to use adjectives in a sentence.
When you use a predicate adjective, you should not decline the adjective.
Predicate adjectives always go to the end of sentences.

Das Auto ist **rot**.   Das Essen schmeckt sehr **gut**.

You can only build very short sentences with these adjectives.

Attributive adjectives are far more important. These adjectives come before the nouns they modify.
Attributive adjectives must be declined. Because there are many ways to decline adjectives, it is recommended that you learn these forms very carefully.
On the next page there is a table that shows the possible ways for adjective declination.

The rules:

weak declination	=	noun with a definite article
mixed declination	=	noun with an indefinite article
strong declination	=	noun without an article

Nominativ / Nominative

Maskulin / masculine	Feminin / feminine	Neutral / neutral
der rote Wagen	die rote Bahn	das rote Auto
ein roter Wagen	eine rote Bahn	ein rotes Auto
roter Wagen	rote Bahn	rotes Auto

Genitiv / Genitive

Maskulin / masculine	Feminin / feminine	Neutral / neutral
des roten Wagens	der roten Bahn	das rote Auto
eines roten Wagens	einer roten Bahn	eines roten Autos
roten Wagens	roter Bahn	roten Autos

Dativ / Dative

Maskulin / masculine	Feminin / feminine	Neutral / neutral
dem roten Wagen	der roten Bahn	dem roten Auto
einem roten Wagen	einer roten Bahn	einem roten Auto
rotem Wagen	roter Bahn	rotem Auto

Akkusativ / Accusative

Maskulin / masculine	Feminin / feminine	Neutral / neutral
den roten Wagen	die rote Bahn	das rote Auto
einen roten Wagen	eine rote Bahn	ein rotes Auto
roten Wagen	rote Bahn	rotes Auto

Plural / Plural

Nominative	Genitive	Dativ e	Accusative
die roten Autos	der roten Autos	den roten Autos	die roten Autos
keine roten Autos	keiner roten Autos	keinen roten Autos	keine roten Autos
rote Autos	roter Autos	roten Autos	rote Autos

2. "keine" and "nicht"

When you make a negative sentence in German, you should recognise the two different methods.

a) You can change the article of a noun to show that a situation or person doesn't exist.

Er hat viel Geld.	Er hat kein Geld.
(He has a lot of money.	*He has no money.)*
Er hat viele Freunde.	Er hat keine Freunde.
(He has many friends.	He has no friends.)

You must always negate a noun in this fashion. Because the word *"kein"* is an article, you must always pay attention to the genus, case und number.

b) The second possibility is to negate the verb. For this you can use the word *"nicht"*.

Sie geht zur Arbeit.	Sie geht nicht zur Arbeit.
(She goes to work.	She doesn't go to work.)
Sie fährt mit dem Auto.	Sie fährt nicht mit dem Auto.
(She travels with the car.	She doesn't travel with the car.)

The word *"nicht"* is not declined or conjugated.

Hinweise / Important information:

Im Restaurant / At a restaurant:

Because there are hardly any differences between quality restaurants in different European countries, it is difficult to depict a visit to a typical German restaurant.

Making a reservation is always recommended, as in Germany it is otherwise likely that you will find all the tables are already taken, even on weekdays.

When you first enter an establishment, you should wait at the reception area until you can tell the host or hostess that you have a reserved table – or if you haven't made a reservation, until a table is found for you.

When you sit at your table, menus will be brought to you, and then you will see that there are hardly any typical German dishes available. The image of Germans eating *"Sauerkraut mit Eisbein"* is something you will likely forget very quickly when you visit a German restaurant.

Or course there will be places – especially in tourist centres – that offer such dishes, but mainly because of tourists. Otherwise, the menus are very international in scope.

There are also many local restaurants where you can also eat, but here the selection is mostly small and the quality of dishes is not especially good.

There are also noticeable regional differences in the quality of the local restaurant. While you can find good food in almost every local restaurant in South Germany – especially in the state of Baden-Württemberg – your chances decrease the further north you go.
Additionally, it is also interesting to try regional dishes offered by local bed and breakfasts.

Also the question of tipping the host follows the international standards. Even though the cost of service is included already in the prices the host expects around 10% of the total as a tip. Only in cases where you believe the service is very bad should you tip less or not at all.

You also certainly have read that Germany is a country of beer drinkers. This is partially true, as you can see from the wide selection of beer types available. You should take advantage of this during your next visit and try a few of these beers.

However, beer is not exclusively consumed in Germany. You also will find many fine wines at restaurants. You should not pass up the opportunity to try a dry "Riesling" from the Rhine valley or from the Mosel river. In recent years, public pressure has won with the result that the quality of German wine has improved dramatically.

Banken und Post

CD2
TOP 10 Changing money is one of the most important tasks that you will do as a tourist in a bank. You will rarely use the bank's other functions, so we will concentrate mainly on that aspect of banking.

The post office plays a more important role, as you will want to buy stamps for your letters and postcards, and also make your phone calls.

Wichtige Formulierungen! / Important formulas!
Listen first to these phrases:

Ich möchte etwas Geld wechseln.	I would like to change some money.
Der Wechselkurs beträgt ...	The exchange rate is...
In welchen Scheinen soll ich Ihnen den Betrag geben?	Which denominations do you want that in?
Können Sie mir sagen, wo das Postamt ist?	Could you please tell me where the post office is?
Hier vorne auf der Kaiserstraße.	Over there, at the beginning of the Kaiserstrasse.
Hier links um die Ecke.	Over there, left, on the corner.
Ich möchte gern zehn Briefmarken kaufen.	I would like to buy ten stamps, please.
Briefmarken für Ansichtskarten nach Japan.	I would like stamps for postcards to Japan, please.
eins, zwei, drei, vier, fünf	one, two, three, four, five
sechs, sieben, acht, neun, zehn	six, seven, eight, nine, ten
elf, zwölf	eleven, twelve
dreizehn, vierzehn, fünfzehn, sechzehn, siebzehn, achtzehn, neunzehn	thirteen, fourteen, fifteen, sixteen, seventeen, eighteen, nineteen
zwanzig, einundzwanzig, zweiundzwanzig	twenty, twenty-one, twenty-two
dreißig, vierzig, fünfzig, sechzig, siebzig, achtzig, neunzig	tthirty, forty, fifty, sixty seventy, eighty, ninety
einhundert, zweihundert, dreihundert	one hundred, two hundred, three hundred

:D2 **Dialog 6 / Dialogue 6**

Now listen to the following dialogue:

Mishiko now goes to a bank to change money, and then she goes to the post office to buy stamps, so that she can write her friends and family in Japan.

Mishiko:
Entschuldigung, können Sie mir bitte sagen, wo ich Geld wechseln kann?

Mishiko:
Excuse me, could you tell me where I can change money?

Passantin:
Da gehen Sie am besten hier über die Straße, dann sehen sie gleich auf der linken Seite eine Sparkasse.

Passer-by:
You should go along the street here, then you will see a savings bank on the left side.

Mishiko:
Herzlichen Dank. Auf Wiedersehen.

Mishiko:
Thank you. Good bye.

Passantin:
Gern geschehen. Auf Wiedersehen.

Passer-by:
Glad to do it. Good bye.

Mishiko betritt die Sparkasse und geht zu dem Schalter mit der Aufschrift: "Sorten".
Mishiko enters the savings bank and goes to the window marked "Currencies."

Mishiko:
Guten Tag, kann ich bei Ihnen Geld wechseln?

Mishiko:
Hello, can I change money here?

Bankangestellter:
Ja, wie viel möchten Sie denn umtauschen?

Bank clerk:
Yes, how much do you want to change?

Mishiko:
Ich hätte gerne 500 DM.

Mishiko:
I would like 500 Marks.

Bankangestellter:
Gerne, zahlen Sie den Betrag bar, oder soll ich ihn lieber von ihrer Kreditkarte abbuchen?

Bank clerk:
No problem. Do you wish to pay in cash, or by credit card?

Mishiko:
Von der Kreditkarte bitte.

Mishiko:
By credit card, please.

Bankangestellter:
In welchen Scheinen soll ich Ihnen denn den Betrag geben?

Bank clerk:
And which denominations do you want?

Mishiko:
Ich hätte gerne drei Einhundert DM Scheine, drei Fünfzig DM Scheine, zwei Zwanzig DM Scheine und einen Zehn DM Schein.

Mishiko:
I would like three one-hundred Mark notes, three fifty Mark notes, two twenty Mark notes and one ten Mark note.

Bankangestellter:
Gern. Einhundert, zweihundert, dreihundert, dreihundertundfünfzig, vierhundert, vierhundertundfünfzig, vierhundertundsiebzig, vierhundertund neunzig, fünfhundert. Bitte schön.

Bank clerk:
Right. One hundred, two hundred, three hundred, three hundred and fifty, four hundred, four hundred and fifty, four hundred and seventy, four hundred and ninety, five hundred. Here you are.

Mishiko:
Vielen Dank.

Mishiko:
Thank you very much.

Bankangestellter:
Bitte schön. Sie können übrigens mit Ihrer Kreditkarte auch an jedem Geldautomaten Geld abholen. Dann sind Sie nicht auf die Öffnungszeiten der Bank angewiesen.

Bank clerk:
You're welcome. You can also use your credit card at any automatic teller machine to get cash. That way, you don't have to worry about banking hours.

Mishiko:
Oh, das wusste ich nicht. Das ist aber ein guter Vorschlag. Vielen Dank.

Mishiko:
Thanks, I didn't know that. That's a good idea.

Bankangestellter:
Bitte. Auf Wiedersehen.

Bank clerk:
You're welcome. Good bye.

Mishiko:
Auf Wiedersehen.

Mishiko:
Good bye.

Mishiko verlässt die Sparkasse und fragt wieder eine Passantin nach dem Weg zum Postamt.
Mishiko leaves the bank and asks another passer-by where she can find the post office.

Mishiko:
Entschuldigung, würden Sie mir bitte sagen, wo ich das nächste Postamt finde?

Mishiko:
Excuse me, could you tell me where the nearest post office is?

Passantin:
Selbstverständlich. Das Postamt ist auf der Kaiserstraße. Sie müssen nur

Passer-by:
Certainly. The post office is on Kaiserstrasse. You only have to cross the intersection, then

die Kreuzung überqueren, dann gehen Sie noch ca. 500 m geradeaus, dann sehen Sie das Postamt auf der linken Seite. Es ist ein rotes Gebäude.	go 500 metres straight ahead, and then you will see the post office on the left side. It's a red building.

Mishiko:
Danke, das werde ich sicher finden.

Mishiko:
Thank you, I'm sure I'll find it.

Mishiko betritt das Postamt und geht zum nächsten freien Schalter.
Mishiko enters the post office and goes to the next available window.

Mishiko:
Guten Tag, kann ich bei Ihnen zehn Briefmarken bekommen?

Mishiko:
Hello. Can I purchase ten stamps, please?

Postangestellter:
Ja, welche Marken möchten Sie denn haben?

Postal clerk:
Yes, which stamps would you like?

Mishiko:
Fünf Marken für Briefe und fünf Marken für Ansichtskarten nach Japan.

Mishiko:
Five stamps for letters and five for postcards to Japan.

Postangestellter:
Dies sind die Marken für die Briefe und dies die Marken für die Ansichtskarten.

Postal clerk:
These are the stamps for the letters, and these are the stamps for the postcards.

Mishiko:
Vielen Dank.

Mishiko:
Thank you.

Postangestellter:
Kann ich sonst noch etwas für sie tun?

Postal clerk:
Is there something else I can do for you?

Mishiko:
Nein, das war alles. Ach, kann ich von hier auch nach Japan telefonieren?

Mishiko:
No, thanks, that was all. Oh, can I also call Japan from here?

Postangestellter:
Ja, sofort am Eingang finden Sie ein Telefon. Von dort aus können Sie auch internationale Gespräche führen.

Postal clerk:
Yes, you can. Right at the entrance you will see a phone. You can make international calls there.

Mishiko:
Danke und tschüss.

Mishiko:
Thanks and good bye.

Postangestellter:
Tschüss.

Postal clerk:
Good bye.

I recommend that you listen to the entire dialogue one more time. You should also repeat the individual sentences so that you can get the right feeling for the correct pronunciation.
(If the dialogue is too fast, please use the pause button on your CD player.)

Übung 1 / Exercise 1

In the following exercise put the sentences in the simple past!

B Beispiel / Example:

Sprecher: *Mishiko geht über die Straße.*
Speaker: *Mishiko goes along the street.*

Sie: *Mishiko ging über die Straße.*
You: *Mishiko went along the street.*

Sprecher: *Mishiko tauscht in der Bank Geld um.*
Speaker: *Mishiko changes money at the bank.*

Sie: *Mishiko tauschte in der Bank Geld um.*
You: *Mishiko changed money at the bank.*

Sprecher: *Mishiko zahlt den Betrag in bar.*
Speaker: *Mishiko pays the bill in cash.*

Sie: *Mishiko zahlte den Betrag in bar.*
You: *Mishiko paid the bill in cash.*

Exercise:

1. Mishiko geht über die Straße.   Mishiko goes along the street.
   Mishiko ging über die Straße.   ***Mishiko went along the street.***

2. Mishiko tauscht in der Bank   Mishiko changes money at the bank.
   Geld um.
   Mishiko tauschte in der   ***Mishiko changed money at the bank.***
   Bank Geld um.

3. Mishiko zahlt den Betrag in bar.   Mishiko pays the bill in cash.
   Mishiko zahlte den Betrag in bar.   ***Mishiko paid the bil in cash.***

4. Mishiko betritt die Sparkasse und geht auf den Schalter zu.
   Mishiko betrat die Sparkasse und ging auf den Schalter zu.

   Mishiko enters the savings bank and goes to the window.
   Mishiko entered the savings bank and went to the window.

5. Die Passantin gibt ihr die gewünschte Auskunft.
   Die Passantin gab ihr die gewünschte Auskunft.

   The passer-by gives her the information she wants.
   The passer-by gave her the information she wanted.

6. Sie erklärt ihr den Weg ganz genau.
   Sie erklärte ihr den Weg ganz genau.

   She explains the way very precisely.
   She explained the way very precisely.

7. Wir schreiben unseren Eltern eine Ansichtskarte aus Deutschland.
   Wie schrieben unseren Eltern eine Ansichtskarte aus Deutschland.

   We are writing our parents a postcard from Germany.
   We wrote our parents a postcard from Germany.

8. Mishiko hebt 500 DM von ihrem Konto ab.
   Mishiko hob 500 DM von ihrem Konto ab.

   Mishiko withdraws 500 Marks from her account.
   Mishiko withdrew 500 Marks from her account.

9. Wir besuchen unsere Freunde in München.
   Wir besuchten unsere Freunde in München.

   We are visiting our friends in Munich.
   We visited our friends in Munich.

10. Herr und Frau Seuthe laden Mishiko zu Essen ein.
    Herr und Frau Seuthe luden Mishiko zum Essen ein.

    Mr. and Mrs. Seuthe invite Mishiko to dinner.
    Mr. and Mrs. Seuthe invited Mishiko to dinner.

11. Ihr fahrt mit dem ICE über Köln nach Wuppertal.
    Ihr fahrt mit dem ICE über Köln nach Wuppertal.

    You take the ICE through Cologne to Wuppertal.
    You took the ICE through Cologne to Wuppertal.

12. Andreas und Herr Lehmann zeigen Mishiko das Hotel.
    Andreas und Herr Lehmann zeigten Mishiko das Hotel.

    Andreas and Mr. Lehmann show Mishiko the hotel.
    Andreas and Mr. Lehmann showed Mishiko the hotel.

13. Mishiko telefoniert mit ihren Eltern in Japan.
    Mishiko telefonierte mit ihren Eltern in Japan.

    Mishiko telephones her parents in Japan.
    Mishiko telephoned her parents in Japan.

14. Der Zug kommt pünktlich in München an.

The train arrives on time in Munich.

Der Zug kam pünktlich in München an.

The train arrived on time in Munich.

15. Ich laufe schnell zur nächsten Sparkasse.

I run quickly to the next savings bank.

Ich lief schnell zur nächsten Sparkasse.

I ran quickly to the next savings bank.

CD2 TOP13 Übung 2 / Exercise 2

You can consider these exercises relaxed, as you only need to repeat the following numbers after the speaker.

B **Beispiel / Example:**

Sprecher:	*fünf*
Speaker:	*five*
Sie:	*fünf*
You:	*five*
Sprecher:	*dreiundsechzig*
Speaker:	*sixty-three*
Sie:	*dreiundsechzig*
You:	*sixty-three*
Sprecher:	*einhundertfünfundneunzig*
Speaker:	*One hundred and ninety-five*
Sie:	*einhundertfünfundneunzig*
You:	*One hundred and ninety-five*

1.
2.
3.

 Exercise:

1. fünf   5
   five   *5*

2. dreiundsechzig   63
   sixty-three   *63*

3. einhundertfünfundneunzig   195
   One hundred and ninety-five   *195*

4. siebenunddreißig   37
 thirty-seven   *37*

5. zweihundertachtzehn   218
 two hundred and eighteen   *218*

6. einhundertelf   111
 One hundred and eleven   *111*

7. eintausendsiebzehn   1017
 One thousand and seventeen   *1017*

8. fünfhundertfünfundfünfzig   555
 five hundred and fifty-five   *555*

CD2 OP14 Übung 3 / Exercise 3

In this exercise you will learn the difference between the words "schon" (earlier than expected) and "erst" (later than expected). First listen to speaker 1, who will give you the practise sentence; then listen to speaker 2, who will give you some additional information. From this additional information you should decide if "erst" or "schon" is the correct choice.

B   Beispiel / Example:

Sprecher 1: *Mishiko ist seit zwei Wochen in Deutschland.*
Speaker 1: *Mishiko has been in Germany for two weeks.*

Sprecher 2: *Das ist nicht lange.*
Speaker 2: *That isn't long.*

Sie: *Mishiko ist erst zwei Wochen in Deutschland.*
You: *Mishiko has been in Germany for two weeks.*

Sprecher 1: *Sie hat in dieser Zeit acht Geschäftsfreunde besucht.*
Speaker 1: *She has visited eight business colleagues during this time.*

Sprecher 2: *Das ist sehr viel.*
Speaker 2: *That is a lot.*

Sie: *Sie hat in dieser Zeit schon acht Geschäftsfreunde besucht.*
You: *She has already visited eight business colleagues.*

Sprecher 1: *Andreas kann morgen nach München fahren.*
Speaker 1: *Andreas can travel to Munich tomorrow.*

Sprecher 2: *Er hat heute keine Zeit.*
Speaker 2: *Today he has no time.*

Sie: *Andreas kann erst morgen nach München fahren.*
You: *Not until tomorrow can Andreas travel to Munich.*

 Exercise:

1. Mishiko ist seit zwei Wochen in Deutschland.
   Das ist nicht lange.
   Mishiko ist erst seit zwei Wochen in Deutschland.

   Mishiko has been in Germany for two weeks.
   That isn't long.
   Mishiko has been in Germany for two weeks.

2. Sie hat in dieser Zeit acht Geschäftsfreunde besucht.
   Das ist sehr viel.
   Sie hat in dieser Zeit schon acht Geschäftsfreunde besucht.

   She has visited eight business colleagues during this time.
   That is a lot.
   She has already visited eight business colleagues.

3. Andreas kann morgen nach München fahren.
   Er hat heute keine Zeit.
   Andreas kann erst morgen nach München fahren.

   Andreas can go to Munich tomorrow.
   Today he has no time.
   Not until tomorrow can Andreas travel to Munich.

4. Andreas kann morgen nach München fahren.
   Er hat einen Termin abgesagt.
   Andreas kann schon morgen nach München fahren.

   Andreas can go to Munich tomorrow.
   He has cancelled an appointment.
   Andreas can travel to Munich as early as tomorrow.

5. Die Sparkasse öffnet um 9:00 Uhr.
   Mishiko ist zu früh dort.
   Die Sparkasse öffnet erst um 9:00 Uhr.

   The savings bank opens at 9:00 a.m.
   Mishiko is there too early.
   The savings bank is open only after 9 a.m.

6. Der Brief ist in fünf Tagen in Japan.
   Das ist eine kurze Zeit.
   Der Brief ist schon in fünf Tagen in Japan.

   The letter takes five days to go to Japan.
   That is very fast.
   The letter takes only five days to get to Japan.

7. Herrn Seuthes Freunde warteten auf ihn.   Mr. Seuthe's friends waited for him.
   Er kam etwas zu spät.   He arrived late.
   Herrn Seuthes Freunde warteten schon auf ihn.   *Mr. Seuthe's friends have been waiting for him.*

8. Der Zug kam um 15:30 Uhr in Wuppertal an.   The train arrived in Wuppertal at 3:30 p.m.
   Er hatte 45 Minuten Verspätung.   It was delayed by 45 minutes.
   Der Zug kam erst um 15:30 Uhr in Wuppertal an.   *The train arrived finally in Wuppertal at 3:30 p.m.*

9. Mishikos Tochter ist jetzt sieben Jahre alt.   Mishikos daughter is seven years old now.
   Das kommt Mishiko sehr alt vor.   That seems very old to Mishiko.
   Mishikos Tochter ist jetzt schon sieben Jahre alt.   *Mishiko's daughter is seven years old now.*

10. Andreas will Herrn Lehmann heute Abend besuchen.   Andreas wants to visit Mr. Lehmann tonight.
    Er wollte eigentlich morgen Abend kommen.   He really wanted to come tomorrow evening.
    Andreas kommt Herrn Lehmann schon heute Abend besuchen.   *Andreas is already visiting Mr. Lehmann tonight.*

11. Der Mann sieht wie Vierzig aus.   The man looks like he is 40 years old.
    Er ist aber erst 30 Jahre alt.   He is, however, only 30.
    Der Mann sieht schon wie Vierzig aus.   *The man already looks like he is 40.*

12. Mishiko fliegt in drei Wochen nach Japan zurück.   Mishiko flies back to Japan in three weeks.
    Sie wollte eigentlich in zwei Wochen zurückfliegen.   She actually wanted to return in two weeks.
    Mishiko fliegt erst in drei Wochen nach Japan zurück.   *Mishiko can only fly back to Japan in three weeks' time.*

Grammatik / Grammar

1. Das Präteritum / Simple past tense

The simple past tense is used mainly in written German. Many Germans prefer the present perfect tense when speaking. However, there are hardly any rules that specify when to use either form.
When you form the simple past, you must know the difference between the strong (irregular) and weak (regular) verbs.

The simple past of weak verbs:

The regular verbs in the simple past are very predictable. You only need to put an ending on the verb, as the verb stem does not change.

	Präsens/Present	Präteritum/Past
machen / do		
ich	mache	machte
du	machst	machtest
er	macht	machte
sie	macht	machte
es	macht	machte
wir	machen	machten
ihr	macht	machtet
sie/Sie	machen	machen

Präsens/Present		Präteritum/Past
zahlen / pay		
ich	zahle	zahlte
du	zahlst	zahltest
er	zahlt	zahlte
sie	zahlt	zahlte
es	zahlt	zahlte
wir	zahlen	zahlten
ihr	zahlt	zahltet
sie/Sie	zahlen	zahlten

The simple past of strong verbs

The simple past of strong verbs is irregular, and the vowel in the verb stem changes. In the appendix you will find a list of the most important strong verbs.

Präsens/Present		Präteritum/Past
kommen / come		
ich	komme	kam
du	kommst	kamst
er	kommt	kam
sie	kommt	kam
es	kommt	kam
wir	kommen	kamen
ihr	kommt	kamt
sie/Sie	kommen	kamen

Präsens/Present		Präteritum/Past
bringen / bring		
ich	bringe	brachte
du	bringst	brachtest
er	bringt	brachte
sie	bringt	brachte
es	bringt	brachte
wir	bringen	brachten
ihr	bringt	brachtet
sie/Sie	bringen	brachten

Because the simple past is created without an auxiliary verb, the sentence structure does not change. For a sentence originally in the present tense, simply change the verb.

2. Zahlwörter / Numerals

Kardinalzahlen (Cardinal numbers)		Ordinalzahlen (Ordinal numbers)
eins	1	ersten
zwei	2	zweiten
drei	3	dritten
vier	4	vierten
fünf	5	fünften
sechs	6	sechsten
sieben	7	siebten
acht	8	achten
neun	9	neunten
zehn	10	zehnten
elf	11	elften
zwölf	12	zwölften
dreizehn	13	dreizehnten
vierzehn	14	vierzehnten
fünfzehn	15	fünfzehnten
zwanzig	20	zwanzigsten
einundzwanzig	21	einundzwanzigsten
dreißig	30	dreißigsten
vierzig	40	vierzigsten
fünfzig	50	fünfzigsten
sechzig	60	sechzigsten
siebzig	70	siebzigsten
achtzig	80	achtzigsten
neunzig	90	neunzigsten
hundert	100	hundertsten
tausend	1000	tausendsten
Millionen	1000000	Millionsten

3. „schon" and „erst"

For the use of these two words there are no rules because these are relative expressions.
Depending on the point of view of the speaker or listener something will appear to be "schon" (earlier than expected) or "erst" (later than expected).

When for example a child "schon vier Jahre alt ist" the parents are saying that their child is growing up quickly. In comparison to an infant, this is correct.
The same parents could also say that "ihr Kind erst vier Jahre alt ist". In this case they are comparing their child to an older one.
With these two words the speaker always expresses his relationship or attitude to the topic being discussed.

Hinweise / Important information:

Banken und Post / At the bank and post office

The number of banks in Germany is very large. In every city you will find a bank where you can obtain cash.
The opening times of the banks vary greatly, however, and so we cannot furnish any standard opening times. One thing we can say is that banks are open longer on Thursdays (to around 6:00 p.m.).
When you want to change money at a bank, turn to the window with the sign that says "Sorten" (foreign currency) or "Devisen" (currency exchange). Here you can change money, cash traveller's cheques or withdraw money with your credit card.
Even when the banks are closed, you can still go to the automatic teller machines which are widespread in Germany, to withdraw cash. Most major credit cards and Eurocheque cards are accepted.

Many post offices also feature automatic teller machines.
Post offices are almost always open from 8:00 a.m. to 6:00 p.m. (Saturdays until 12:00 p.m.). Here you can purchase stamps and make phone calls.

4. Geld / Money

The German monetary system is decimal, which means that 1 DM is worth 100 Pfennig. Prices can also be listed decimally, for example 3,45 DM. (spoken as: »drei Mark fünfundvierzig«)

There are the following coins:

1 Pf	10 Pf	2 DM
2 Pf	50 Pf	5 DM
5 Pf	1 DM	

There are the following bank notes:

5 DM	100 DM
10 DM	200 DM
20 DM	500 DM
50 DM	1000 DM

Schriftliche Übung / Written exercise:

Put these sentences in past tense!

1. Die Sparkasse schließt um 17:00 Uhr.

Die Sparkasse _____ um 17:00 Uhr.

2. Mishiko kommt heute Morgen nach München.

Mishiko _____ heute Morgen nach München.

3. Herr Seuthe will seinen Freund in Wuppertal besuchen.

Herr Seuthe _____ seinen Freund in Wuppertal besuchen.

4. Die Geschäftsfreunde treffen sich in einem Restaurant.

Die Geschäftsfreunde _____ sich in einem Restaurant.

5. Das Postamt öffnet um 18:00 Uhr.

Das Postamt _____ um 18:00 Uhr.

6. Andreas und Herr Seuthe gehen vor dem Essen spazieren.

Andreas und Herr Seuthe _____ vor dem Essen spazieren.

7. Sie suchen einen Platz am Fenster.

Sie _____ einen Platz am Fenster.

8. Sie können an der Tankstelle mit Ihrer Kreditkarte bezahlen.

Sie _____ an der Tankstelle mit Ihrer Kreditkarte bezahlen.

9. Wir nehmen den 500 DM Schein nicht an.

Wir _____ den 500 DM Schein nicht an.

10. Andreas und Mishiko lernen sich in Köln kennen.

Andreas und Mishiko _____ sich in Köln kennen.

Lektion **7**

Im Hotel

Reserving a room, arriving at a hotel and making requests and complaints at a hotel are definitely situations you will encounter when travelling in foreign countries.
In this lesson you will learn important information on these subjects.

Wichtige Formulierungen! / Important phrases:
Listen first to these important phrases:

Haben Sie noch Zimmer frei?	Do you have a room available?
Zwei Einzelzimmer für drei Nächte.	Two single rooms for three nights.
Ein Doppelzimmer für ein Wochenende.	A double room for one weekend.
Hat das Zimmer Dusche oder Bad?	Does the room have a shower or bath?
Ich möchte gern ein ruhiges Zimmer.	I would like a quiet room.
Um wie viel Uhr gibt es Frühstück?	What time is breakfast?
Können Sie mich bitte wecken?	Could you give me a wake-up call?
Wo befindet sich der Frühstücksraum?	Where is the breakfast room?
Wie teuer ist ein Doppelzimmer?	How much is a double room?
Hier sind Ihre Zimmerschlüssel.	Here is your room key.
Ihr Zimmer befindet sich auf der sechsten Etage.	Your room is on the sixth floor.
Sie können auch den Aufzug benutzen.	You can also take the lift.
Gibt es ein Telefon auf dem Zimmer?	Is there a phone in the room?
Können Sie mir bitte die Rechnung fertig machen?	Could you give me the bill, please?
Wir möchten gern abreisen.	We would like to depart.
Das ist ziemlich teuer.	That's rather expensive.
Können Sie mir ein Restaurant empfehlen?	Could you recommend a restaurant?
Können Sie mir Karten für das Theater reservieren?	Could you reserve tickets for the theatre for me?
Würden Sie mir bitte ein Taxi bestellen?	Would you please order me a taxi?
Haben Sie einen Hotelsafe?	Do you have a hotel safe?

Dialog 7 / Dialogue 7

Now listen to the following dialogue:

Mishiko's business partner would like to invite her for a short trip to the Alps. He reserves the hotel rooms by telephone.

Geschäftspartner:
Guten Tag, ist dort das Hotel Edelweiß?

Business partner:
Hello, is that the Hotel Edelweiß?

Hotelangestellte:
Ja. Guten Tag. Was kann ich für Sie tun?

Hotel clerk:
Yes, it is. What can I do for you?

Geschäftspartner:
Ich möchte gerne für das nächste Wochenende zwei Einzel- und ein Doppelzimmer reservieren. Haben Sie noch etwas frei?

Business partner:
I would like to reserve two single rooms and a double room for next weekend. Are there any vacancies?

Hotelangestellte:
Einen Augenblick. Ja, am nächsten Wochenende haben wir noch freie Zimmer.

Hotel clerk:
Just a minute. Yes, we have vacancies for next weekend.

Geschäftspartner:
Das ist schön. Wie teuer sind denn die Zimmer?

Business partner:
That's good. How expensive are the rooms?

Hotelangestellte:
Ein Einzelzimmer kostet 120 DM und das Doppelzimmer kostet 210 DM.

Hotel clerk:
A single room costs 120 DM, and a double costs 210 DM.

Geschäftspartner:
Das ist aber ziemlich teuer. Haben die Zimmer auch alle Dusche oder Bad?

Business partner:
That's rather expensive. Do the rooms have showers or baths?

Hotelangestellte:
Selbstverständlich haben alle Zimmer eine Dusche.

Hotel clerk:
Of course, all rooms have showers.

Geschäftspartner:
Gut. Dann möchte ich gern zwei Einzel- und ein Doppelzimmer reservieren.

Business partner:
OK. Then I would like to reserve two single rooms and one double room.

Hotelangestellte: Auf welchen Namen bitte?	*In whose name, please?*
Geschäftspartner: Wehrmeier.	*Business partner:* Wehrmeier.
Hotelangestellte: Gut, Herr Wehrmeier. Ihre Zimmer sind reserviert. Wann werden Sie ungefähr anreisen?	*Hotel clerk:* Right, Mr. Wehrmeier, your rooms are reserved. When do you think you will arive?
Geschäftspartner: Wir werden am Freitag gegen 17:00 Uhr bei Ihnen sein.	*Business partner:* We will arrive on Friday at about 5 p.m.
Hotelangestellte: Schönen Dank. Auf Wiederhören.	*Hotel clerk:* Thank you. Good bye.
Geschäftspartner: Auf Wiederhören.	*Business partner:* Good bye.

The guests arrive at the hotel.

Geschäftspartner: Guten Tag, ich habe zwei Einzel- und ein Doppelzimmer auf den Namen "Wehrmeier" reserviert.	*Business partner:* Hello, I have a reservation for two single and one double room under the name Wehrmeier.
Hotelangestellte: Ja, Guten Tag Herr Wehrmeier. Zwei Einzel- und ein Doppelzimmer bis Sonntag. Hier sind ihre Schlüssel. Die Zimmer befinden sich auf der sechsten Etage. Sie können dort den Aufzug benutzen.	*Hotel clerk:* Yes, hello Mr. Wehrmeier. Two single and one double room until Sunday. Here are your keys. The rooms are on the sixth floor. You can take the lift.
Geschäftspartner: Schön. Wann gibt es Frühstück?	*Business partner:* Great. When is breakfast served?
Hotelangestellte: Sie können von 7:00 Uhr bis 10:00 Uhr frühstücken.	*Hotel clerk:* Breakfast is served from 7 a.m. until 10 a.m.
Geschäftspartner: Wo ist der Frühstücksraum?	*Business partner:* And where is the breakfast room?
Hotelangestellte: Hier links. Sofort die erste Tür.	*Hotel clerk:* Right over here, first door on the left.

Geschäftspartner:
Würden Sie uns bitte um 8:00
Uhr wecken?

Business partner:
I would like an wake-up call at 8:00.

Hotelangestellte:
Selbstverständlich, Herr Wehrmeier.
Sie werden um 8:00 Uhr geweckt.

Hotel clerk:
Certainly, Mr. Wehrmeier. You will be woken
at 8 a.m.

Geschäftspartner:
Schönen Dank. Ach, haben die
Zimmer auch Telefon?

Business partner:
Thank you very much. Oh, does the room
also have a phone?

Hotelangestellte:
Ja, alle Zimmer verfügen über
einen Telefonanschluss.

Hotel clerk:
Yes, all rooms have phones, sir.

Geschäftspartner:
Oh, mir fällt noch etwas ein.
Können Sie für uns Karten für
das Theater reservieren?

Business partner:
Oh, something else — could you reserve
tickets at the theatre for us?

Hotelangestellte:
Vier Karten für die Vorstellung
heute Abend?

Hotel clerk:
Four tickets for the performance tonight?

Geschäftspartner:
Ja bitte.

Business partner:
Yes, please.

Hotelangestellte:
Ich bestelle die Karten für Sie.

Hotel clerk:
I'll order the tickets for you, sir.

Geschäftspartner:
Danke. Und bitte ein Taxi für 19:00 Uhr.

Business partner:
Thank you. And could you also get me
a taxi for 7 p.m.?

Hotelangestellte:
Gern.

Hotel clerk:
Certainly, sir.

**Die Kollegen haben ein paar schöne Urlaubstage verbracht und müssen nun
leider wieder nach München zurück.**
*The colleagues have now spent a few nice days vacationing and must now return
to Munich.*

Geschäftspartner:
Wir möchten morgen abreisen.
Würden Sie uns bitte die Rechnung
fertig machen?

Business partner:
We would like to leave tomorrow.
Would you please give me the bill?

Hotelangestellte:
Ja, Herr Wehrmeier. Möchten
Sie sofort oder erst morgen zahlen?

Hotel clerk:
Certainly, Mr. Wehrmeier. Would you like
to pay now or tomorrow?

Geschäftspartner:
Ich zahle sofort.

Business partner:
I'll pay now.

Hotelangestellte:
Ihre Rechnung bitte.

Hotel clerk:
Your check, sir.

Geschäftspartner:
Kann ich auch mit der Kreditkarte
bezahlen?

Business partner:
Could I also pay with a credit card?

Hotelangestellte:
Aber sicher.

Hotel clerk:
Certainly.

Geschäftspartner:
Auf Wiedersehen.

Business partner:
Good bye.

Hotelangestellte:
Schönen Dank. Gute Heimreise.

Hotel clerk:
Thank you. Have a nice trip.

I recommend that you listen to the entire dialogue one more time. You should also repeat the individual sentences so that you can get the right feeling for the correct pronunciation.
(If the dialogue is too fast, please use the pause button on your CD player.)

CD3 / OP3 Übung 1 / Exercise 1

Please link both the main sentence clauses you will hear with each other to make a sentence with a main and a subordinate clause.
Use the subordinating conjunctions "weil" (because) or "obwohl" (although).

 Beispiel / Example:

Sprecher:	*Wir machen einen Kurzurlaub.*	
	Wir haben drei Tage frei.	
Speaker:	*We are taking a short holiday.*	
	We have three days free.	

Sie: *Weil wir drei Tage frei haben, machen wir einen Kurzurlaub.*

You: *Because we have three days free, we are taking a short holiday.*

Sprecher: *Familie Lehmann geht spazieren. Es regnet sehr stark.*
Speaker: *The Lehmanns are going walking. It is raining very heavily.*

Sie: *Obwohl es sehr stark regnet, geht Familie Lehmann spazieren.*
You: *Although it is raining very heavily, the Lehmanns are going walking.*

Sprecher: *Andreas kam zu spät in München an. Der Zug hatte Verspätung.*
Speaker: *Andreas arrived late in Munich. The train was delayed.*

Sie: *Weil der Zug Verspätung hatte, kam Andreas zu spät in München an.*

You: *Because the train was delayed, Andreas arrived late in Munich.*

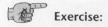 **Exercise:**

1. Wir machen einen Kurzurlaub.
Wir haben drei Tage frei.
Weil wir drei Tage frei haben,
machen wir einen Kurzurlaub.

   We are taking a short holiday.
We have three days free.
Because we have three days free, we are
taking a short holiday.

2. Familie Lehmann geht spazieren.
Es regnet sehr stark.
Obwohl es sehr stark regnet,
geht Familie Lehmann spazieren.

   The Lehmanns are going walking.
It is raining very heavily.
Although it is raining very heavily,
the Lehmanns are going walking.

3. Andreas kam zu spät in München an.
Der Zug hatte Verspätung.
Weil der Zug Verspätung hatte,
kam Andreas zu spät in
München an.

   Andreas arrived late in Munich.
The train was delayed.
Because the train was delayed,
Andreas arrived late in Munich.

4. Wir reservieren ein Doppelzimmer
im Hotel Edelweiß.
Das Zimmer ist sehr teuer.
Obwohl das Zimmer sehr teuer
ist, reservieren wir ein
Doppelzimmer im Hotel Edelweiß.

   We are reserving a double room at
the Hotel Edelweiß.
The room is very expensive.
Although the room is very expensive,
we are reserving a double room at
the Hotel Edelweiß.

5. Das Zimmer ist in der sechsten Etage.
Wir benutzen keinen Aufzug.
Obwohl das Zimmer in der
sechsten Etage ist, benutzen
wir keinen Aufzug.

   The room is in the sixth floor.
We are not using the elevator.
Although the room is on the sixth floor,
we are not using the elevator.

6. Die Geschäftsfreunde wollen
heute Abend ins Theater gehen.
Sie bestellen ein Taxi.
Weil die Geschäftsfreunde heute
Abend ins Theater gehen wollen,
bestellen sie ein Taxi.

   The business partners want to go the
theatre tonight.
They are ordering a taxi.
Because the business partners want to
go the theatre tonight, they are ordering
a taxi.

7. Die Hotelgäste haben Urlaub.
Sie lassen sich um 7:00 Uhr
wecken.
Obwohl die Hotelgäste Urlaub
haben, lassen sie sich um
7:00 Uhr wecken.

The hotel guests are on holiday.
They are arranging a wake-up call
for 7 a.m.
Although the hotel guests are on holiday,
they are arranging a wake-up call
for 7 a.m.

8. Mishiko bestellt ein Menü
mit fünf Gängen.
Sie hat großen Hunger.
Weil Mishiko großen Hunger hat,
bestellt Sie ein Menü
mit fünf Gängen.

Mishiko is ordering a five-course meal.

She is very hungry.
Because Mishiko is very hungry, she
is ordering a five-course meal.

9. Das Hotelzimmer ist sehr ruhig.
Es liegt an einer Hauptstraße.
Obwohl das Hotelzimmer an
einer Hauptstraße liegt, ist es
sehr ruhig.

The hotel room is very quiet.
It is on a main street.
Although the hotel room is on a
main street, it is very quiet.

10. Herr Seuthe bittet um die Rechnung.
Er will morgen früh abreisen.
Weil Herr Seuthe morgen früh
abreisen will, bittet er um
die Rechnung.

Mr. Seuthe is asking for the bill.
He wants to depart early tomorrow.
Because Mr. Seuthe wants to depart
early tomorrow, he is asking for
the bill.

CD2 Übung 2 / Exercise 2
TOP 17

In this exercise you should transform a compound sentence with a main and
subordinate clause using the subordinate conjunction "weil" (because) to a
compound sentence using the subordinate conjunction "da.".
Please keep in mind that when you use "da" the subordinate clause comes
first in the sentence.

B Beispiel / Example:

Sprecher: *Andreas kam zu spät in München an,*
weil der Zug Verspätung hatte.

Speaker: *Andreas arrived late in Munich because*
the train was delayed.

Sie: *Da der Zug Verspätung hatte, kam Andreas*
zu spät in München an.

You: *Because the train was delayed, Andreas*
arrived late in Munich.

Sprecher: *Wir machen einen kurzen Urlaub, weil wir drei Tage frei haben.*
Speaker: *We are taking a short holiday because we had three days free.*

Sie: *Da wir drei Tage frei haben, machen wir einen kurzen Urlaub.*
You: *Because we had three days free, we are taking a short holiday.*

Sprecher: *Wir sind heute zu Hause geblieben, weil es so stark*
geregnet hat.

Speaker: *We have stayed home today because it has been*
raining so hard.

Sie: *Da es so stark geregnet hat, sind wir heute zu Hause geblieben.*
You: *Because it has been raining so hard, we have stayed*
home today.

 **Exercise:**

1. Andreas kam zu spät in München an, weil der Zug Verspätung hatte.
   Andreas arrived late in Munich because the train was delayed.
   Da der Zug Verspätung hatte, kam Andreas zu spät in München an.
   Because the train was delayed, Andreas arrived late in Munich.

2. Wir machen einen kurzen Urlaub, weil wir drei Tage frei haben.
   We are taking a short holiday because we had three days free.
   Da wir drei Tage frei haben, machen wir einen kurzen Urlaub.
   Because we had three days free, we are taking a short holiday.

3. Wir sind heute zu Hause geblieben, weil es so stark geregnet hat.
   We have stayed home today because it has been raining so hard.
   Da es so stark geregnet hat, sind wir heute zu Hause geblieben.
   Because it has been raining so hard, we have stayed home today.

4. Die Hotelzimmer sind sehr teuer, weil das Hotel sehr viel Komfort hat.
   The hotel rooms are very expensive because the hotel is very comfortable.
   Da das Hotel sehr viel Komfort hat, sind die Hotelzimmer sehr teuer.
   Because the hotel is very comfortable, the rooms are very expensive.

5. Ich konnte dich gestern nicht besuchen, weil ich einen dringenden Termin beim Arzt hatte.
   I couldn't visit you yesterday because I had an urgent doctor's appointment.
   Da ich einen dringenden Termin beim Arzt hatte, konnte ich dich gestern nicht besuchen.
   Because I had an urgent doctor's appointment, I couldn't visit you yesterday.

6. Herr Lehmann bezahlte mit seiner Kreditkarte, weil er nicht genug Bargeld hatte.
   Mr. Lehmann is paying with his credit card because he doesn't have enough cash.
   Da er nicht genug Bargeld hatte, bezahlte Herr Lehmann mit seiner Kreditkarte.
   Because he doesn't have enough cash, Mr. Lehmann is paying with his credit card.

7. Wir können morgen bis 10:00 Uhr schlafen, weil wir Ferien haben.
Da wir Ferien haben, können wir morgen bis 10:00 Uhr schlafen.

We will be able to sleep to 10 tomorrow morning because we are on holiday.
Because we are on holiday, we will be able to sleep to 10 tomorrow morning.

8. Mishiko saß vorgestern den ganzen Tag im Hotelzimmer, weil sie auf einen Anruf aus Tokio wartete.
Da sie auf einen Anruf aus Tokio wartete, saß Mishiko vorgestern den ganzen Tag im Hotelzimmer.

The day before yesterday, Mishiko sat in her hotel room the whole time because she was waiting for a call from Tokyo.
Because she was waiting for a call from Tokyo, Mishiko sat in her hotel room the whole time, the day before yesterday.

9. Sie fuhren mit dem Taxi zum Theater, weil sie sonst zu spät gekommen wären.
Da sie sonst zu spät gekommen wären, fuhren sie mit dem Taxi zum Theater.

They went by taxi to the theatre because otherwise they would have been too late.
Because they otherwise would have been too late, they went by taxi to the theatre.

Grammatik / Grammar

1. Kausale Nebensätze mit "weil" und "da" /
Causal subordinate clauses with "weil" (because) and "da" (because):

The conjunctions "weil" and "da" are almost identical grammatically and in meaning. Both are used to give the reason for the action in the main clause. The only difference between these two conjunctions is that the subordinate clause that begins with "da" will mostly form the beginning of a sentence. This rule is not mandatory, but it has become common and should be observed. Subordinate clauses with "weil" can come at the beginning, middle or at the end. The main rule is that the most important information should be at the front of the sentence.

Beispiel / Example:

Er kann heute nicht kommen, weil er keine Zeit hat.
(He can't come today because he has no time.)

Weil er keine Zeit hat, kann er heute nicht kommen.
(Because he has no time, he can't come today.)

Er kann, weil er keine Zeit hat, heute nicht kommen.
(He cannot come today because he has no time.)

Da er keine Zeit hat, kann er heute nicht kommen.
(Because he has no time, he can't come today.)

When you want to insert the subordinate clause with "weil" in the main clause, you should put it directly after the verb in the main clause. (Only by doing this can your be sure that your sentence is grammatically correct.)

115

2. Konzessive Nebensätze mit "obwohl" /
Concessive subordinate clauses with "obwohl" (although):

Subordinate clauses with "obwohl" are always used when you want to give an argument against doing something – exactly like the conjunction "although". When you describe an action that has no real reason then you use the conjunction "obwohl".

Beispiel / Example:

> Die Kinder spielen draußen, obwohl es regnet.
> *(The children are playing outside, although it is raining.)*

The subordinate clause with "obwohl" can come at the beginning, middle or at the end of the sentence.

> *Die Kinder spielen draußen, obwohl es regnet.*

> *Obwohl es regnet, spielen die Kinder draußen.*

> *Die Kinder spielen, obwohl es regnet, draußen.*

Also in this case you should put the subordinate clause directly after the verb in the main clause.

3. Nebensätze allgemein /
Subordinate clauses in general:

When you create a subordinate clause, you should always keep in mind that the conjugated verb comes last in the clause.
This rule is always true.

> Andreas ruft im Hotel an.
> *(Andreas is calling the hotel)*

> Er will ein Doppelzimmer reservieren.
> *(He wants to reserve a double room)*

Andreas ruft im Hotel an, weil er ein Doppelzimmer reservieren will.

Hinweise / Important information:

Übernachten in Deutschland / Accommodation in Germany

The accommodation possibilities in Germany are not any different than those you have experienced in other countries.

The "Jugendherbergen" (youth hostels), are interesting for youthful travellers, because with these you can stay the night for a low price.

The quality of the youth hostels varies dramatically. There are very simple ones, that offer little comfort, but especially in large cities there are youth hostels that are quite comfortable. (The prices also vary a lot.)

The most important thing is to have a valid International Youth Hostel membership card "Jugendherbergs-Ausweis". You can also buy these in the youth hostels themselves.

Other budget accommodations are available at guest-houses. Here you normally get a simple room, but most also have a shower and toilet. Guest-houses are often smaller houses with a very limited number of beds.

The ratings system of hotels in the different categories is the same as the international standard.

Depending on your budget, you have a choice ranging from simple guest-houses up to international luxury hotels.

When you would like to reserve a room in a big city or in a popular tourist region, it is recommended that you phone ahead to reserve a room.

At many hotels it is possible to book a room through the Internet.

Schriftliche Übung / Written exercises:

Insert either "weil" or "obwohl" in the blank spaces.

1) Sie fragen den Angestellten nach einem Hotelzimmer, _____ sie nicht reserviert haben.

2) Mishiko hat nur einen kleinen Koffer, _____ sie nur zwei Tage bleiben möchte.

3) Herr Lehmann verzichtete auf den Nachtisch, _____ er Angst um seine Figur hat.

4) Andreas macht ein paar Tage Urlaub, _____ er sehr viel Arbeit zu erledigen hat.

5) Herr Seuthe kam noch rechtzeitig in München an, _____ der Zug Verspätung hatte.

6) Es wird gleich regnen, _____ der Himmel schon ganz dunkel ist.

7) Mishiko muss heute den ganzen Tag im Bett bleiben, _____ sie krank ist.

8) Herr Seuthe geht zur Arbeit, _____ er starke Kopfschmerzen hat.

9) Wie bekamen noch ein Hotelzimmer, _____ das Hotel sehr stark besucht war.

10) Andreas möchte nicht nach Japan reisen, _____ er kein Japanisch kann.

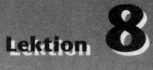

Einen Ausflug mit dem Auto planen

CD3
TOP5 In this lesson you will learn some information about Germany and about the German history and culture.

Along with this information that you will need when you drive in Germany, you will also get to know some famous tourist attractions.

Because the weather is an important factor for every trip, you will also hear and read expressions on this topic.

Wichtige Formulierungen! / Important phrases!
Listen first to these important phrases:

Der Wetterbericht sagt, dass das Wetter gut wird.	The weather report predicts good weather.
Es soll jedenfalls nicht regnen.	It will not rain.
Wo sollen wir denn hinfahren?	Where should we drive?
Mir gefällt Norddeutschland sehr gut, weil wir dort ans Meer können.	I like North Germany a lot because we can go to the sea coast.
Ich würde gern in die "Neuen Bundesländer" fahren.	I would like to travel through the former East German states.
Wenn wir nach Bayern fahren, können wir einen Abstecher in die Alpen machen.	When we go to Bavaria we can make a detour through the Alps.
Wir müssen zuerst zur Tankstelle fahren.	We have to go to a petrol station first.
Unser Auto muss Super bleifrei tanken.	Our car uses Super Lead-Free only.
Ich lasse noch den Ölstand kontrollieren.	I will have the oil checked.
Der Reifendruck ist in Ordnung.	The tyre pressure is ok.
Sollen wir über die Autobahn oder über die Landstraße fahren?	Should we take the motorway or the scenic route?
An der nächsten Ausfahrt müssen wir abfahren.	We have to get off at the next exit.
Auf dieser Straße dürfen wir nur 100 km/h fahren.	The speed limit on this street is only 100 km/h.
Dieses Dorf ist wirklich sehr schön und alt.	This town is really very old and quite pretty.
Dort ist auch unser Hotel.	Our hotel is also there.

CD3 TOP6 **Dialog 8 / Dialogue 8**

Now listen to the following dialogue:

Mishiko, Andreas, Herr Seuthe und Frau Seuthe planen einen Ausflug. Sie möchten mit dem Auto eine Tour durch Deutschland machen. Sie sprechen gerade darüber, wohin sie fahren werden.
Mishiko, Andreas and Mr. and Mrs. Seuthe are planning a trip. They would like to drive through Germany. They are discussing where they want to go.

Andreas:
Der Wetterbericht sagt, dass das Wetter in ganz Deutschland gut wird. Es soll jedenfalls nicht regnen. Deshalb ist es egal, wohin wir fahren.

Andreas:
The weather report predicts the weather in all of Germany will be fine. It won't rain at any rate, so it won't matter where we go.

Mishiko:
Ich würde gerne in die "Neuen Bundesländer" fahren. Diese Gegend kenne ich noch gar nicht.

Mishiko:
I would like to go to the former East German states. I don't know that region at all.

Frau Seuthe:
In Norddeutschland ist es auch sehr schön, da können wir ans Meer fahren. Die Nordsee gefällt mir nämlich sehr gut.

Mrs. Seuthe:
It is also quite pretty in North Germany, because we can drive to the sea. I like the North Sea a lot.

Herr Seuthe:
Das ist richtig, aber wenn wir nach Bayern fahren, können wir auch einen Abstecher in die Alpen machen. Das wäre für Mishiko auch sehr interessant.

Mr. Seuthe:
That's true, but if we go to Bavaria, we can also make a detour to the Alps. I think that would be very interesting for Mishiko.

Andreas:
Da Mishiko unser Gast ist, soll sie entscheiden, wohin wir fahren.

Andreas:
Because Mishiko is our guest, she should decide where we will go.

Mishiko:
Danke. Ich würde sehr gern nach Weimar in Thüringen und nach Dresden in Sachsen fahren. Wäre euch das auch recht?

Mishiko:
Thank you. I would like to visit Weimar in Thuringia and Dresden in Saxony. Would that be ok with you?

Frau Seuthe:
Das ist eine gute Idee. Diese beiden Städte kenne ich auch noch nicht.

Mrs. Seuthe:
That's a good idea. I've never been to either city.

121

Herr Seuthe: Gut, dann sollten wir jetzt die Route planen. Sollen wir auch schon Zimmer reservieren?	*Mr. Seuthe:* Right, then we should decide on which route to take. Should we also make reservations at a hotel?
Andreas: Ich glaube, dass das in der Nebensaison nicht notwendig ist. Wir sollten es so probieren.	*Andreas:* I think that that won't be necessary during the off-season. We should just go there and see.
Herr Seuthe: Was meint ihr, sollen wir über die Autobahn oder über die Bundesstraßen fahren?	*Mr. Seuthe:* What do you all think? Should we go on the motorway or on the normal roads?
Frau Seuthe: Wir sollten bis Weimar auf der Autobahn fahren, das geht viel schneller. Von Weimar bis Dresden können wir ja Bundesstraßen nehmen.	*Mrs. Seuthe:* We should take the motorway to Weimar because it's much quicker. From Weimar to Dresden we can take the back roads.
Andreas: Gut, so sollten wir es machen. Dann können wir ja gleich morgen Vormittag starten.	*Andreas:* Right, so let's do it. That means we can start tomorrow morning.
Herr Seuthe: Ich muss zuerst zur Tankstelle fahren. Das kann ich ja gleich erledigen.	*Mr. Seuthe:* I have to go first to a petrol station, so I'll get that done now.

An der Tankstelle; Herr Seuthe tankt während ihn der Tankwart fragt:
At the petrol station, Mr. Seuthe fills up his car and the attendant asks him:

Tankwart: Soll ich den Ölstand und den Reifendruck kontrollieren?	*Petrol attendant:* Should I check the oil and tyres?
Herr Seuthe: Ja, der Ölstand muss kontrolliert werden. Der Reifendruck ist in Ordnung.	*Mr. Seuthe:* Yes, the oil has to be checked. The tyre pressure is fine.

Am nächsten Morgen beginnt für die vier Freunde die Reise.
The next morning the four friends begin their trip.

Mishiko:
Ich freue mich schon sehr auf Weimar.

Mishiko:
I'm looking forward to Weimar.

Frau Seuthe:
Gleich sind wir dort. An der nächsten
Ausfahrt müssen wir abfahren.

Mrs. Seuthe:
We're almost there. We have to take
the next exit.

Andreas:
Pass auf, auf dieser Straße darf man
nur 100 km/h fahren.

Andreas:
Watch out, this street has a speed limit
of only 100 km/h.

Herr Seuthe:
Oh, das habe ich gar nicht gesehen.

Mr. Seuthe:
Oh! I didn't notice that at all.

Mishiko:
Dort ist ja schon das Ortsschild
von Weimar.

Mishiko:
There is the city limit sign for Weimar.

Frau Seuthe:
Jetzt müssen wir nur noch unser
Hotel suchen.

Mrs. Seuthe:
Now we need to find our hotel.

Andreas:
Hier auf dieser Straße muss unser
Hotel liegen. Dort kann ich es
auch schon sehen.

Andreas:
Our hotel must be on this street. There!
I can already see it.

CD3 **I recommend that you listen to the entire dialogue one more time. You**
TOP7 **should also repeat the individual sentences so that you can get the right**
feeling for the correct pronunciation.
(If the dialogue is too fast, please use the pause button on your CD player.)

Übung 1 / Exercise 1

Put the sentences you hear into passive:

B **Beispiel / Example:**

Sprecher:	*Der Tankwart kontrolliert den Ölstand.*
Speaker:	*The attendant is checking the oil.*
Sie:	*Der Ölstand wird kontrolliert.*
You:	*The oil level is being checked.*
Sprecher:	*Andreas reserviert ein Hotelzimmer.*
Speaker:	*Andreas is reserving a hotel room.*
Sie:	*Ein Hotelzimmer wird reserviert.*
You:	*A hotel room is being reserved.*
Sprecher:	*Der Hotelangestellte gibt*
	Mishiko den Zimmerschlüssel.
Speaker:	*The hotel clerk is giving Mishiko the room key.*
Sie:	*Der Zimmerschlüssel wird Mishiko gegeben.*
You:	*The hotel key is being given to Mishiko.*

☞ **Exercise:**

1. Der Tankwart kontrolliert den Ölstand.
   The attendant is checking the oil.
   Der Ölstand wird kontrolliert.
   The oil level is being checked.

2. Andreas reserviert ein Hotelzimmer.
   Andreas is reserving a hotel room.
   Ein Hotelzimmer wird reserviert.
   A hotel room is being reserved.

3. Der Hotelangestellte gibt Mishiko den Zimmerschlüssel.
   The hotel clerk is giving Mishiko the room key.
   Der Zimmerschlüssel wird Mishiko gegeben.
   The hotel key is being given to Mishiko.

4. Andreas hat den Reifendruck überprüft.
   Andreas checked the tyre pressures.
   Der Reifendruck ist überprüft worden.
   The tyre pressures were checked.

5. Herr Seuthe bezahlte gestern die Hotelrechnung.
   Mr. Seuthe paid the hotel bill yesterday.
   Die Hotelrechnung wurde gestern bezahlt.
   The hotel bill was paid yesterday.

6. Die vier Freunde haben die Reiseroute sorgfältig geplant.
   The four friends planned the travel route carefully.
   Die Reiseroute ist sorgfältig geplant worden.
   The travel route was carefully planned.

7. Der Tankwart hilft Herrn Seuthe.
   The attendant is helping Mr. Seuthe.
   Herrn Seuthe wird geholfen.
   Mr. Seuthe is being helped.

8. Mishiko hat dem Freund geantwortet.
   Mishiko answered the friend.
   Dem Freund ist geantwortet worden.
   The friend was answered.

9. Ich hoffe, daß der Mechaniker das Auto repariert.
   I hope the mechanic repairs the car.
   Ich hoffe, dass das Auto repariert wird.
   I hope the car is repaired.

10. Er fragt seinen Freund, ob er morgen kommt.
    He asks his friend if he is coming tomorrow.
    Sein Freund wird gefragt, ob er morgen kommt.
    His friend is asked if he is coming tomorrow.

CD3 Übung 2 / Exercise 2
TOP8

Now put the sentences you hear in the active form:

B Beispiel / Example:

Sprecher: *Der Reifendruck ist vom Mechaniker überprüft worden.*

Speaker: *The tyre pressure was checked by the mechanic.*

Sie: *Der Mechaniker hat den Reifendruck überprüft.*

You: *The mechanic checked the tyre pressure.*

Sprecher: *Herrn Seuthe wird vom Tankwart geholfen.*

Speaker: *Mr. Seuthe is being helped by the attendant.*

Sie: *Der Tankwart hilft Herrn Seuthe.*

You: *The attendant is helping Mr. Seuthe.*

Sprecher: *Weimar wird von vielen Touristen besucht.*

Speaker: *Weimar is visited by many tourists.*

Sie: *Viele Touristen besuchen Weimar.*

You: *Many tourists visit Weimar.*

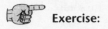 **Exercise:**

1. Der Reifendruck ist vom
   Mechaniker überprüft worden.
   Der Mechaniker hat den
   Reifendruck überprüft.

   The tyre pressure was checked by
   the mechanic.
   The mechanic checked the tyre
   pressure.

2. Herrn Seuthe wird vom
   Tankwart geholfen.
   Der Tankwart hilft Herrn Seuthe.

   Mr. Seuthe is being helped by
   the attendant.
   The attendant is helping Mr. Seuthe.

3. Weimar wird von vielen
   Touristen besucht.
   Viele Touristen besuchen Weimar.

   Weimar is visited by many tourists.

   Many tourists visit Weimar.

4. Die Information ist von der
   Hotelangestellten gegeben worden.
   Die Hotelangestellte hat die
   Information gegeben.

   The information was provided by
   the hotel clerk.
   The hotel clerk provided
   the information.

5. Die Reiseroute wurde von den
   Freunden geplant.
   Die Freunde planten die
   Reiseroute.

   The travel route was planned by the
   friends.
   The friends planned the travel route.

6. Ich hoffe, dass das Buch von
   den Leuten gelesen wird.
   Ich hoffe, daß die Leute
   das Buch lesen.

   I hope that the book will be read.

   I hope that people will read the book.

7. Die Beschwerde ist von Andreas eingereicht worden.

   Andreas hat die Beschwerde eingereicht.

   The complaint was made by Andreas.

   Andreas made the complaint.

8. Die Reise wurde Mishiko von ihren Freunden geschenkt.

   Die Freunde schenkten Mishiko die Reise.

   The holiday trip was a gift to Mishiko from her friends.

   The friends gave Mishiko a holiday trip as a gift.

9. Das Verkehrsschild ist von dem Autofahrer übersehen worden.

   Der Autofahrer hat das Verkehrsschild übersehen.

   The traffic sign was overlooked by the driver.

   The driver overlooked the traffic sign.

10. Das Auto war von Herrn Seuthe aufgetankt worden.

    Herr Seuthe hatte das Auto aufgetankt.

    The car was filled up by Mr. Seuthe.

    Mr. Seuthe filled up the car.

Grammatik / Grammar

Das Passiv / The Passive

The transformation of sentences from active to passive is very regular in German and simple to learn.
When you want to make such a transformation, you must follow the following rules:

1. First find the direct (accusative) object of the active sentence.

2. Put the accusative object in the nominative case.

3. Put the conjugated form of the auxiliary verb "werden" at the second position in the passive sentence.

4. Create the past participle of the main verb.

5. Put this past participle at the very end of the sentence.

6. Leave out the nominative noun or pronoun of the passive sentence.

7. All other parts of the sentence are unchanged when put into the passive.

Beispiel / Example:

> Der Tankwart überprüft heute Morgen den Reifendruck.
> *(The attendent will check the tyre pressure this morning.)*

1. "den Reifendruck" is the accusative or direct object.

2. "Der Reifendruck" is the nominative form.

3. "Der Reifendruck wird ..." is the conjugated form of the verb "werden"

4. "überprüft" is the past participle of the verb "überprüfen" (check)

5. "Der Reifendruck wird überprüft."

6. "Der Reifendruck wird heute Morgen überprüft."

All transformations follow the same principle. Please keep in mind that you can only transform sentences that have an accusative object.
If you want to transform a sentence that has only a dative object, you can also follow this rule, taking into account one exception.

The dative object is also included in the passive sentence. It takes the first position in the sentence, but it remains in the dative case.

> Der Mechaniker hilft dem Mann.
> *(The mechanic is helping the man.)*

> Dem Mann wird geholfen.
> *(The man is being helped.)*

Of course you must also take into account the verb tense of the active sentence when you wish to make a transformation. You can create passive sentences with every verb tense.

Along with the simple present tense you have already learned, in this lesson you will be introduced to the simple past and the present perfect forms.

Präteritum / Simple past

The simple past is only a little bit different from the present. You only have to put the auxiliary verb "werden" into the past tense (wurde).

> Der Mechaniker überprüfte der Reifendruck.
> *(The mechanic checked the tyre pressure)*
>
> Der Reifendruck wurde überprüft.
> *(The tyre pressure was checked.)*

Perfekt / Present perfect

When you want to make a passive sentence with present perfect, you need an auxiliary verb. In contrast to the active sentences, where you must choose either the auxiliary verbs "haben" or "sein", you can make passive sentences with "sein". (the only exceptions are the modal verbs that must use "haben".)

The conjugated form of "sein" comes second in the sentence. At the next-to-last position of the passive sentence you put the past participle of the main verb; the end position is taken by the past participle of the auxiliary verb "werden" ("worden").

> Der Mechaniker hat den Reifendruck überprüft.
> *(The mechanic checked the tyre pressure.)*
>
> Der Reifendruck ist überprüft worden.
> *(The tyre pressure was checked.)*

Please keep in mind that sentences that take neither an accusative nor a dative object cannot be transformed to passive.

Hinweise / Important information:

Die sechzehn deutschen Bundesländer / The sixteen German states:

Germany is a federation with sixteen states. Each state has its own capital with its own government.
All laws relating to the politics of the states, are decided by these state governments.

Here is a list of the sixteen states and their capitals:

Schleswig-Holstein	Kiel
Mecklenburg-Vorpommern	Schwerin
Hamburg	Hamburg
Bremen	Bremen
Berlin	Berlin
Brandenburg	Potsdam
Niedersachsen	Hannover
Sachsen-Anhalt	Magdeburg

Nordrhein-Westfalen	Düsseldorf
Hessen	Wiesbaden
Thüringen	Erfurt
Sachsen	Dresden
Rheinland-Pfalz	Mainz
Saarland	Saarbrücken
Baden-Württemberg	Stuttgart
Bayern	München

Schriftliche Übung / Written exercise

Create the simple past and present perfect of the following passive sentences

1. Das Auto wird an der Tankstelle gewaschen.
   The car is cleaned at the petrol station.

   Simple past _____

   Present perfect _____

2. Andreas wird von Herrn Lehmann geholfen.
   Andreas is being helped by Mr. Lehmann.

   Simple past _____

   Present perfect _____

3. Der Zimmerschlüssel wird den Hotelgästen gegeben.
   The room's key is given to the guests of the hotel.

   Simple past _____

   Present perfect _____

4. Weimar wird von vielen Touristen besucht.
   Weimar is visited by many tourists.

   Simple past _____

   Present perfect _____

Freizeit
Theater- oder Kinobesuch

During your stay in Germany, you will also want to take advantage of the wide selection of leisure activities.
In this lesson you will learn how to plan a visit to the theatre, cinema or concert.

Wichtige Formulierungen! / Important phrases:
First, listen to these phrases:

Können Sie mir sagen, wo ich ein Kinoprogramm bekomme?	Can you please tell me where I can find a cinema listing?
Welcher Film läuft in der Spätvorstellung?	What is the late show?
Wann beginnt der Hauptfilm?	When does the main film begin?
Ab wie viel Jahren ist der Film freigegeben?	What is the film rated?
Ich hätte gern zwei Karten für die Spätvorstellung.	I would like two tickets for the late show, please.
Welche Aufführung gibt es im Schauspielhaus?	Which play is being staged at the theatre?
Bekomme ich als Student eine Ermäßigung?	Can I get a student discount?
Wo kann ich das Programmheft bekommen?	Where can I get a programme?
Geben Sie Ihren Mantel bitte an der Garderobe ab.	Please leave your overcoat at the cloakroom.
Ich hätte gern zwei Karten für die dritte Reihe.	I would like two tickets for the third row, please.
Getränke bekommen Sie in der Pause im Foyer.	You can purchase refreshments in the lobby during the interval.
Im Konzertsaal wird die Dritte Symphonie von Beethoven gespielt.	Beethoven's Third Symphony will be performed at the concert hall.
Gibt es für das Konzert noch Karten?	Are there still tickets available for the concert?
Die Konzerte werden in der Stadthalle gegeben.	The concert will be performed in the civic auditorium.
Mit den Eintrittskarten können Sie auch die öffentlichen Verkehrsmittel benutzen.	These tickets also allow you to use all available means of public transport.

D3 Dialog 9 / Dialogue 9
OP2

Now listen to the following dialogue:

Mishiko und Andreas wollen den Abend gemeinsam verbringen.
Sie wissen noch nicht, ob sie ins Kino, Theater oder Konzert gehen sollen.
Sie sind im Informationsbüro, um sich nach den Möglichkeiten zu erkundigen.
Mishiko and Andreas want to go out for the evening.
They don't know if they should go to the cinema, theatre or a concert.
They go to a tourist information bureau to find out what options they have.

Andreas:
Können Sie mir sagen, wo ich das Kinoprogramm bekomme?

Andreas:
Could you tell me please where I can find a theatre programme?

Angestellte:
Ein Kinoprogramm kann ich Ihnen geben. Bitte, hier sind alle Kinos der Stadt aufgeführt.

Clerk:
I can give you a cinema programme. Here you are. All the cinemas in the city are listed here.

Andreas:
Danke schön.

Andreas:
Thank you.

Mishiko:
Welcher Film läuft denn in der Spätvorstellung?

Mishiko:
What is the late night film?

Andreas:
Dort läuft "Titanic", aber den Film kenne ich schon.

Andreas:
"Titanic" but I've already seen it.

Mishiko:
"Titanic" kenne ich auch. Was läuft denn als Hauptfilm?

Mishiko:
I've also seen "Titanic".
What is the main feature?

Andreas:
"Der Pferdeflüsterer".

Andreas:
"The Horse Whisperer".

Mishiko:
Wann beginnt der Hauptfilm?

Mishiko:
What time does the main film begin?

Andreas:
Um 20:15 Uhr.

Andreas:
At 8:15 p.m.

Mishiko:
Wir sollten auch fragen, was im
Schauspielhaus aufgeführt wird.

Angestellte:
Im Schauspielhaus können Sie heute
Abend "Iphigenie auf Tauris" von
Johann Wolfgang von Goethe sehen.

Andreas:
Das ist sehr interessant. Ein typisches
Drama der deutschen Klassik.

Mishiko:
Ich glaube, dafür ist mein Deutsch
nicht gut genug. Da müsste ich zuerst
das Stück lesen, um es besser
zu verstehen.

Andreas:
Schade, es hätte dir bestimmt gut
gefallen. Vielleicht wird aber auch
ein gutes Konzert in der Stadthalle
gegeben. Können Sie mir sagen, was
heute in der Stadthalle gespielt wird?

Angestellte:
Im Konzertsaal der Stadthalle wird
heute die Dritte Symphonie von
Ludwig van Beethoven gespielt.

Mishiko:
Lass uns bitte in dieses Konzert gehen.
Das interessiert mich sehr.

Andreas:
Einverstanden, dazu habe ich auch Lust.
Geben Sie uns bitte zwei Karten
für das Konzert.

Angestellte:
Hier bitte, zwei Karten für die Stadthalle.
Das kostet 120 DM.

Mishiko:
We should also find out what is playing at
the theatre.

Clerk:
Tonight, Johann Wolfgang von Goethe's play
"Iphigenie auf Tauris" is playing.

Andreas:
That's very interesting. It is a classic German
drama.

Mishiko:
I don't think my German is good enough.
I think I should read the play, so I can better
understand it.

Andreas:
That's too bad. You would definitely have liked
it. Perhaps there's a good concert in the civic
auditorium. Could you please tell me what is
being performed in the civic auditorium?

Clerk:
At the civic auditorium Beethoven's Third
Symphony is being performed.

Mishiko:
Let's go to the concert. It looks very
interesting.

Andreas:
Agreed. I think so too. Two tickets for the
concert, please.

Clerk:
Here you are, two tickets for the civic
auditorium. That comes to 120 DM.

Andreas:
Schönen Dank. Auf Wiedersehen.

Angestellte:
Bitte, gern geschehen. Auf Wiedersehen.

Andreas:
Thank you. Good bye.

Clerk:
You're welcome, glad to do it. Good bye.

Mishiko und Andreas betreten die Stadthalle.
Mishiko and Andreas visit the civic auditorium.

Angestellter:
Geben Sie ihre Mäntel bitte an der Garderobe ab.

Clerk:
Please leave your coats in the cloakroom.

Andreas:
Wo finde ich die Garderobe?

Andreas:
Excuse me, where is the cloakroom?

Angestellter:
Gleich hier um die Ecke.

Clerk:
Over there, just around the corner.

Andreas:
Geben Sie mir bitte ein Programmheft. Können wir auch etwas zu trinken bekommen?

Andreas:
I would like a programme, please. Could we also get some drinks?

Angestellter:
Hier das Programmheft. In der Pause können Sie im Foyer Getränke bekommen.

Clerk:
Here is your programme. During the interval break you can purchase drinks in the foyer.

Andreas:
Schönen Dank.

Andreas:
Thank you.

I recommend that you listen to the entire dialogue one more time. You should also repeat the individual sentences so that you can get the right feeling for the correct pronunciation.
(If the dialogue is too fast, please use the pause button on your CD player.)

CD3 TOP 11 Übung 1 / Exercise 1

Please transform the main sentences you hear into sentences in the Subjunctive II in German.

B Beispiel / Example:

Sprecher: *Mishiko kann das Drama nicht verstehen.*
Sie hat das Stück nicht gelesen.
Speaker: *Mishiko is not able to understand the play.*
She has not read the play.

Sie: *Wenn Mishiko das Stück gelesen hätte,*
könnte sie das Drama verstehen.
You: *If Mishiko had read the play, she would*
be able understand it.

Sprecher: *Mishiko und Andreas bekommen keinen Platz im Theater.*
Sie haben keine Plätze reserviert.
Speaker: *Mishiko and Andreas could not get tickets to the theatre.*
They had made not reservations.

Sie: *Wenn Mishiko und Andreas Plätze reserviert hätten, bekämen*
sie einen Platz im Theater.
You: *If Mishiko and Andreas had made reservations, they would*
have got tickets to the theatre.

Sprecher: *Das Konzert fällt aus. Die Opernsängerin ist erkrankt.*
Speaker: *The concert was cancelled. The opera diva is ill.*

Sie: *Wenn die Opernsängerin nicht erkrankt wäre,*
fiele das Konzert nicht aus.
You: *Were the opera diva not ill, the concert would have not*
been cancelled.

Exercises:

1. Mishiko kann das Drama nicht
verstehen.
Sie hat das Buch nicht gelesen.
Wenn Mishiko das Buch gelesen
hätte, könnte sie das Drama
verstehen.

Mishiko is not able to
understand the play.
She has not read the play.
If Mishiko had read the play, she
would be able understand it.

2. Mishiko und Andreas bekommen
keinen Platz im Theater.
Sie haben keine Plätze reserviert.
Wenn Mishiko und Andreas
Plätze reserviert hätten, bekämen
sie einen Platz im Theater.

Mishiko and Andreas could not get
tickets to the theatre.
They had made not reservations.
If Mishiko and Andreas had made
reservations, they would have got
tickets to the theatre.

3. Das Konzert fällt aus.
Die Opernsängerin ist erkrankt.
Wenn die Opernsängerin nicht
erkrankt wäre, fiele das Konzert
nicht aus.

The concert was cancelled
The opera diva is ill.
Were the opera diva not ill,
the concert would have not
been cancelled.

4. Sie kommen zu spät zur Vorstellung.
Der Bus hat Verspätung.
Wenn der Bus keine Verspätung
hätte, kämen sie nicht zu spät
zur Vorstellung.

They are late for the performance.
The bus was delayed.
If the bus were not delayed, they
would not be late for the performance.

5. Mishiko und Andreas fahren
nicht mit dem Auto.
Es ist defekt.
Wenn das Auto nicht defekt wäre,
führen Mishiko und Andreas
mit ihm.

Mishiko and Andreas are not
taking the car.
It is broken.
If the car were not broken, Mishiko
and Andreas would take it.

6. Herr und Frau Seuthe gehen
nicht spazieren.
Es regnet sehr stark.
Wenn es nicht sehr stark regnete,
gingen Herr und Frau Seuthe
spazieren.

Mr. and Mrs. Seuthe are not going
for a walk.
It is raining very heavily.
If it were not raining heavily, Mr.
and Mrs. Seuthe would go for a walk.

7. Andreas kam uns nicht besuchen.
Er hatte keine Zeit.
Wenn Andreas Zeit gehabt hätte,
wäre er uns besuchen
gekommen.

Andreas didn't visit us.
He had not the time
If Andreas had had time, he would
have visited us.

8. Mishiko ist nicht in ihr
Hotelzimmer gekommen.
Sie hat den Schlüssel verlegt.
Wenn Mishiko den Schlüssel
nicht verlegt hätte, wäre sie
in ihr Hotelzimmer gekommen.

Mishiko didn't go to her hotel room.

She has lost the key.
If Mishiko had not lost the key, she
would have gone to her hotel room.

9. Ich kann ihnen nicht helfen.
Ich muss dringend zur Arbeit.
Wenn ich nicht dringend zur
Arbeit müsste, könnte
ich ihnen helfen.

I can't help you.
I need to go to work urgently.
If I didn't need to go to work so
urgently, I could help you.

10. Die Angestellte reserviert
keine Theaterkarten.
Es gibt keine freien Plätze mehr.
Wenn es noch freie Plätze gäbe,
reservierte die Angestellte
die Theaterkarten.

The clerk didn't reserve any tickets.

There are no tickets available.
If there were still tickets available,
the clerk would reserve tickets.

Übung 2 / Exercise 2

Transform the sentences you hear into Subjunctive II.

B **Beispiel / Example:**

Sprecher: *Ich reserviere kein Hotelzimmer.*
Speaker: *I am not reserving a hotel room.*

Sie: *Ich würde kein Hotelzimmer reservieren.*
You: *I would not reserve a hotel room.*

Sprecher: *Ich fahre nicht mit dem Auto.*
Speaker: *I am not driving my car.*

Sie: *Ich führe nicht mit dem Auto.*
You: *I would not drive my car.*

Sprecher: *Ich lasse das Auto reparieren.*
Speaker: *I am having my car repaired.*

Sie: *Ich ließe das Auto reparieren.*
You: *I would have my car reparied.*

 Exercises:

1. Ich reserviere kein Hotelzimmer.
   Ich würde kein Hotelzimmer reservieren.

   I am not reserving a hotel room.
   I would not reserve a hotel room.

2. Ich fahre nicht mit dem Auto.
   Ich führe nicht mit dem Auto.

   I am not driving my car.
   I would not drive my car.

3. Ich lasse das Auto reparieren.
   Ich ließe das Auto reparieren.

   I am having my car repaired.
   I would have my car repaired.

4. Ich besuche meine Freunde in Köln.
   Ich würde meine Freunde in Köln besuchen.

   I am visiting my friends in Cologne.
   I would visit my friends in Cologne.

5. Er bestellt die Eintrittskarten   He is ordering the tickets for the late
   für die Spätvorstellung.   movie.
   Er würde die Eintrittskarten   *He would order the tickets for the late*
   für die Spätvorstellung bestellen.   *movie.*

6. Andreas geht heute Abend mit   Andreas is going with Mishiko for a
   Mishiko spazieren.   walk tonight.
   Andreas ginge heute Abend   *Andreas would go with Mishiko for a*
   mit Mishiko spazieren.   *walk tonight.*

7. Wir können morgen gemeinsam   We can go together to the theatre
   ins Theater gehen.   tomorrow.
   Wir könnten morgen gemeinsam   *We could go together to the theatre*
   ins Theater gehen.   *tomorrow.*

8. Ihr dürft hier sitzen bleiben.   You can stay seated here.
   Ihr dürftet hier sitzen bleiben.   *You could stay seated here.*

9. Herr und Frau Seuthe kommen   Mr. and Mrs. Seuthe are coming
   schon wieder zu spät.   late again.
   Herr und Frau Seuthe kämen   *Mr. and Mrs. Seuthe could be*
   schon wieder zu spät.   *coming late again.*

10. Ich habe den Film nicht gesehen.   I haven't seen the film.
    Ich hätte den Film nicht   *I would not have seen the film.*
    gesehen.

Grammatik / Grammar

Der Konjunktiv II / The Subjunctive II

When you want to form the subjunctive II in German, you must always take into account two possibilities.

The strong *(irregular)* verbs have a unique tense form in Subjunctive II.
With the weak verbs the subjunctive II is often the same as the simple past.

In the following list you can see these forms.
Always keep in mind that the subjunctive II is based on the simple past of the verbs.

starke Verben / strong verbs (laufen – to run)

	Präteritum simple past	Konjunktiv II subjunctive II
ich laufe	lief	liefe
du läufst	liefst	liefest
er läuft	lief	liefe
sie läuft	lief	liefe
es läuft	lief	liefe
wir laufen	liefen	liefen
ihr lauft	lieft	liefet
sie/Sie laufen	liefen	liefen

As you can see, there is a chance of confusing the simple past and subjunctive II with the strong verbs only in the first and third person plural.

schwache Verben / weak verbs (machen – to make)

	Präteritum simple past	Konjunktiv II subjunctive II
ich mache	machte	machte
du machst	machtest	machtest
er macht	machte	machte
sie macht	machte	machte
es macht	machte	machte
wir machen	machten	machten
ihr macht	machtet	machtet
sie/Sie machen	machten	machten

The forms of the subjunctive II in all conjugations are the same as with the simple past. Because it is easy to confuse the two forms, you should in this case create the subjunctive II with *"würde"*.
There are set rules for written German for when you use the form with *"würde"*.
When you are in Germany, you will quickly notice that very few Germans use the subjunctive without *"würde"*. When you are not sure about a particular verb, you should use the form with *"würde"*.
Please keep in mind that *"würde"* is an auxiliary verb. The main verb must be put at the end of the sentence in the infinitive form.

> Ich käme dich besuchen.
> *I would visit you.*

> Ich würde dich besuchen kommen.

Now look at the subjunctive II of the auxiliary verbs *"haben"* and *"sein"*:

	Präteritum simple past	Konjunktiv II subjunctive II
ich habe	hatte	hätte
du hast	hattest	hättest
er hat	hatte	hätte
sie hat	hatte	hätte
es hat	hatte	hätte
wir haben	hatten	hätten
ihr habt	hattet	hättet
sie/Sie haben	hatten	hätten

	Präteritum simple past	Konjunktiv II subjunctive II
ich bin	war	wäre
du bist	warst	wärest
er ist	war	wäre
sie ist	war	wäre
es ist	war	wäre
wir sind	waren	wären
ihr seid	wart	wäret
sie/Sie sind	waren	wären

With these two auxiliary verbs it is always easy to distinguish the Subjunctive II from the simple past.

The auxiliary verb are always necessary when you want to express something in the past in subjunctive II.

Andreas hat Mishiko eingeladen.
Andreas invited Mishiko.

Andreas hätte Mishiko eingeladen.
Andreas could have invited Mishiko.

Hinweise / Important information:

In every large German city you will find a variety of cultural activities. No matter if you want to go to the cinema, theatre or to a concert, you will find something of interest.
It is best to go to the tourist information office, because here you can find listings of almost every cultural event in the area.

It is usually not necessary to reserve tickets at the cinema, as long as you want to see a popular film that has been showing for a while.
With theatre and concerts it is advisable, however, to reserve tickets at least a couple of days in advance. Often these performances sell out.

Schriftliche Übung / Written exercises:

Put the following verbs in the Subjunctive II:

1. laufen   ich _____

2. gehen   wir _____

3. machen   ihr _____

4. kommen   er _____

5. vergessen   ich _____

6. bestellen   du _____

7. reservieren   wir _____

8. besuchen   Sie _____

9. verlieren   ich _____

10. sehen   du _____

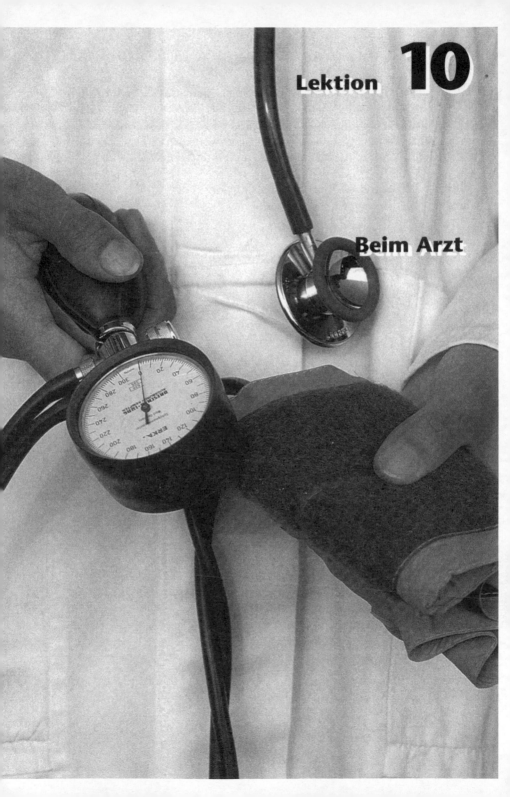

Beim Arzt

CD4
TOP1 It is definitely an uncomfortable event when one falls ill and has to visit a
doctor in a foreign country – especially during one's holiday. In this lesson
you will learn some important vocabulary for such a situation.
In addition I would like to explain the German health care system. Finally, you
can also find out how and where you can purchase medicines in Germany.

Wichtige Formulierungen! / Important phrases:
First, listen to these phrases:

Du solltest besser zum Arzt gehen.	You had better go to the doctor.
Ich hätte gerne einen Termin beim Arzt.	I would like an appointment with the doctor.
Wir sind eine Praxis für Allgemein Medizin.	This is a general practitioner's surgery.
Nehmen Sie bitte im Wartezimmer Platz.	Please take a seat in the waiting room.
Der Nächste bitte!	Next, please!
Ich habe eine Erkältung.	I have a cold.
Mein Hals tut mir weh.	I have a sore throat.
Ihre Mandeln sind entzündet.	My tonsils are sore.
Ich werde Ihnen Antibiotika verschreiben.	I'll prescribe you an antibiotic.
Nehmen Sie täglich eine Tablette.	Take one tablet daily.
Morgens vor dem Frühstück.	In the morning before breakfast.
Das Rezept bekommen Sie bei der Sprechstundenhilfe.	You can pick up your prescription at the reception.
Gute Besserung.	Get well soon.
Haben Sie einen Auslandskrankenschein?	Do you have a foreign insurance ID card?
Ist das der richtige Krankenschein?	Is this the right insurance card?
Wo finde ich die nächste Apotheke?	Where is the nearest chemist?
Gleich hier vorne rechts.	Right over there, to the right.
Was kann ich für Sie tun?	What can I do for you?
Ich möchte dieses Rezept abgeben.	I would like this prescription filled.
Muss ich dafür etwas bezahlen?	Do I have to pay for that?
Ja, Sie müssen 9 DM für das Medikament zuzahlen.	Yes, the medicine costs 9 DM.

D4 Dialog 10 / Dialogue 10
OP2

Now listen to the following dialogue:

Mishiko fühlt sich schon seit ein paar Tagen nicht wohl. Sie hustet sehr und klagt über starke Halsschmerzen. Heute hat sie ihre Stimme fast völlig verloren.
Mishiko has been feeling unwell for a couple of days. She is coughing a lot and has a very sore throat. Today she has almost completely lost her voice.

Andreas:
Guten Morgen, Mishiko. Mit deiner
Erkältung wird es ja immer schlimmer.
Du solltest besser zum Arzt gehen.

Andreas:
Good morning, Mishiko. Your cold seems
to be getting worse. You really should go
to a doctor.

Mishiko:
Ja, obwohl ich das im Ausland
nicht gerne mache.

Mishiko:
Yes, although I don't like to go in a foreign
country.

Andreas:
Das verstehe ich. Trotzdem rufst
du am besten gleich beim Arzt an.
Ich kenne einen gute Praxis für
Allgemein Medizin.

Andreas:
Yes, I understand, but you should call
a doctor anyway.
I know of a good general practitioner.

Mishiko:
Dann gib mir bitte die Telefonnummer.

Mishiko:
All right, can I have the phone number, please?

Andreas:
Ich habe sie schon gefunden. Hier, bitte.

Andreas:
I have it right here.

Mishiko geht sofort zum Telefon und ruft bei dem Arzt an.
Mishiko goes to the phone and calls the doctor immediately.

Sprechstundenhilfe:
Praxis Dr. Senyüz. Was kann
ich für Sie tun?

Receptionist:
Dr. Senyüz's surgery. What can I do
for you?

Mishiko:
Guten Tag. Hier spricht Mishiko Thai.
Ich hätte gerne einen Termin beim Arzt.
Ich fühle mich nicht wohl.

Mishiko:
Hello. my name is Mishiko Thai,
and I would like an appointment.
I feel unwell.

Sprechstundenhilfe:
Wenn es dringend ist, kommen Sie am
besten heute Nachmittag um 16:00 Uhr.

Receptionist:
If it's an emergency, the doctor can see you
today at 4:00 this afternoon.

Mishiko:
Schönen Dank, bis heute Nachmittag.
Auf Wiederhören.

Mishiko:
Thank you, I'll see you this afternoon.
Good bye.

Sprechstundenhilfe:
Auf Wiederhören.

Receptionist:
Good bye.

Mishiko kommt pünktlich zum vereinbarten Termin in die Arztpraxis.
Mishiko comes on time to the doctor's surgery for her appointment.

Mishiko:
Guten Tag, mein Name ist Thai.
Ich habe heute Morgen angerufen und
einen Termin für 16:00 Uhr bekommen.

Mishiko:
Hello, my name is Mishiko Thai.
I called earlier today and set an appointment
for 4:00.

Sprechstundenhilfe:
Guten Tag. Frau Thai, nehmen Sie bitte
im Wartezimmer Platz. Ich werde
Sie gleich aufrufen.

Receptionist:
Hello.Mrs. Thai, will you please take a seat
in the waiting room? I'll call out your
name soon.

Sprechstundenhilfe:
Der Nächste bitte! Frau Thai, würden
Sie bitte in das Zimmer 1 gehen?

Receptionist:
Next please! Mr. Thai, would you please
go to room 1?

Arzt:
Guten Tag, was kann ich für Sie tun?

Doctor:
Hello, what can I do for you?

Mishiko:
Ich habe eine Erkältung. Seit ein paar
Tagen muss ich husten, und außerdem
tut mein Hals sehr weh.

Mishiko:
I have a cold. I've been coughing for a
couple of days and I also have a very sore
throat.

Arzt:
Ich werde nachschauen. Öffnen Sie
bitte Ihren Mund. Das sieht nach
einer Mandelentzündung aus. Sie wären
besser schon etwas früher zu
mir gekommen.

Doctor:
Let me have a look.
Please open your mouth.
That looks like tonsillitis.
You should have come to me sooner.

Mishiko:
Ich dachte, es wäre nur eine
kleine Erkältung.

Mishiko:
I thought it was only a slight cold.

Arzt:
Ich werde Ihnen Antibiotika verschreiben.
Nehmen Sie täglich eine Tablette, am
besten morgens vor dem Frühstück.

Doctor:
I'll prescribe you some antibiotics.
Take one tablet daily, preferably in the
morning before breakfast.

Mishiko:
Ja, wie lange soll ich die Tabletten
nehmen?

Mishiko:
Ok, and how long should I continue
with the tablets?

Arzt:
Wenn es nach vier Tagen nicht besser
ist, kommen Sie bitte wieder in
meine Praxis.

Doctor:
If it doesn't get better after four days,
please come back and see me.

Mishiko:
Ich hoffe, dass es dann ausgeheilt ist.

Mishiko:
I hope it'll be gone by then.

Arzt:
Das Rezept bekommen Sie bei der
Sprechstundenhilfe. Gute Besserung.

Doctor:
You can pick up the prescription at the
receptionist's desk. Hope you feel better soon.

Mishiko:
Danke. Auf Wiedersehen.

Mishiko:
Thank you. Good bye.

Arzt:
Auf Wiedersehen.

Doctor:
Good bye.

Mishiko:
Der Arzt hat gesagt, dass ich
bei Ihnen mein Rezept bekomme.

Mishiko:
The doctor said that I could pick up the
prescription here.

Sprechstundenhilfe:
Ja, Frau Thai. Hier, bitte. Haben Sie
einen Auslandskrankenschein?

Receptionist:
Certainly, Mrs. Thai. Here you are.
Do you have an insurance card?

Mishiko:
Hier bitte. Ist das der richtige
Krankenschein?

Mishiko:
Here you are. Is this the correct health
insurance card?

Sprechstundenhilfe:
Ja, das ist in Ordnung. Auf Wiedersehen
und gute Besserung.

Receptionist:
Yes, that is correct.
Good bye and get well soon!

Mishiko:	*Mishiko:*
Danke. Auf Wiedersehen. Können Sie mir bitte sagen, wo ich die nächste Apotheke finde?	Thank you. Good bye. Could you tell me where the nearest chemist is?
Sprechstundenhilfe:	*Receptionist:*
Gleich hier vorne rechts ist eine Apotheke.	There's one over here on the right.

Mishiko geht zur Apotheke, um ihr Rezept abzugeben.
Mishiko goes to the chemist to fill her prescription.

Mishiko:	*Mishiko:*
Guten Tag, ich möchte dieses Rezept abgeben.	Hello, I would like to have this prescription filled, please.
Apothekerin:	*Pharmacist:*
So, bitte.	Right. Here you are.
Mishiko:	*Mishiko:*
Muss ich dafür etwas bezahlen?	Is there any charge for this?
Apothekerin:	*Pharmacist:*
Ja, Sie müssen 9 DM für das Medikament zuzahlen.	Yes, there is a 9 DM charge for the medicine.
Mishiko:	*Mishiko:*
Schönen Dank. Auf Wiedersehen.	Thank you. Good bye.
Apothekerin:	*Pharmacist:*
Auf Wiedersehen.	Good bye.

I recommend that you listen to the entire dialogue one more time. You should also repeat the individual sentences so that you can get the right feel for the correct pronunciation.
(If the dialogue is too fast, please use the pause button on your CD player.)

Übung 1 / Exercise 1

Please put the sentence you hear in the simple future I:

B Beispiel / Example:

Sprecher: *Mishiko geht zum Arzt.*
Speaker: *Mishiko goes to the doctor.*

Sie: *Mishiko wird zum Arzt gehen.*
You: *Mishiko will go to the doctor.*

Sprecher: *Mishiko ist wieder gesund.*
Speaker: *Mishiko is healthy again.*

Sie: *Mishiko wird wieder gesund sein.*
You: *Mishiko will be healthy again.*

Sprecher: *Die Sprechstundenhilfe gibt Mishiko*
das Rezept.
Speaker: *The receptionist gives Mishiko the prescription.*

Sie: *Die Sprechstundenhilfe wird Mishiko das Rezept geben.*
You: *The receptionist will give Mishiko the prescription.*

Exercise:

1. Mishiko geht zum Arzt.
   Mishiko wird zum Arzt gehen.

   Mishiko goes to the doctor.
   Mishiko will go to the doctor.

2. Mishiko ist wieder gesund.
   Mishiko wird wieder gesund sein.

   Mishiko is healthy again.
   Mishiko will be healthy again.

3. Die Sprechstundenhilfe gibt
   Mishiko das Rezept.
   Die Sprechstundenhilfe wird
   Mishiko das Rezept geben.

   The receptionist gives Mishiko
   the prescription.
   The receptionist will give Mishiko
   the prescription.

4. Andreas empfiehlt Mishiko, zum
   Arzt zu gehen.
   Andreas wird Mishiko empfehlen,
   zum Arzt zu gehen.

   Andreas recommends that Mishiko
   goes to the doctor.
   Andreas will recommend that Mishiko
   goes to the doctor.

5. Der Arzt verschreibt ihr Antibiotika.
   Der Arzt wird ihr Antibiotika verschreiben.

   The doctor prescribes her an antibiotic.
   The doctor will prescribe her an antibiotic.

6. Sie müssen die Tabletten täglich nehmen.
   Sie werden die Tabletten täglich nehmen müssen.

   You have to take the tablets daily.
   You will have to take the tablets daily.

7. In vier Tagen sind Sie bestimmt wieder gesund.
   In vier Tagen werden Sie bestimmt wieder gesund sein.

   In four days you are definitely healthy again.
   In four days you will be definitely healthy again.

8. Mishiko setzt sich ins Wartezimmer.
   Mishiko wird sich ins Wartezimmer setzen.

   Mishiko sits in the waiting room.
   Mishiko will sit in the waiting room.

9. Bei den Tabletten muss man 9 DM zuzahlen.
   Bei den Tabletten wird man 9 DM zuzahlen müssen.

   The tablets cost 9 DM.
   The tablets will cost 9 DM.

10. Mishiko legt ihren internationalen Krankenschein vor.
    Mishiko wird ihren internationalen Krankenschein vorlegen.

    Mishiko shows her international health insurance card.
    Mishiko will show her international health insurance card.

11. Andreas begleitet Mishiko zum Arzt.
    Andreas wird Mishiko zum Arzt begleiten.

    Andreas goes with Mishiko to the doctor.
    Andreas will go with Mishiko to the doctor.

12. Die Kinder ziehen sich bei dem kalten Wetter warm an.
    Die Kinder werden sich bei dem kalten Wetter warm anziehen.

    The children dress warm for the cold weather.
    The children will dress warm for the cold weather

13. Ihr geht am besten direkt zur Apotheke.
    Ihr werdet am besten direkt zur Apotheke gehen.

    You should go straight to the chemist.
    You should go straight to the chemist.

14. Herr und Frau Seuthe fahren im nächsten Jahr nach Japan.
Herr und Frau Seuthe werden im nächsten Jahr nach Japan fahren.

Mr. and Mrs. Seuthe are going to Japan next year.
Mr. and Mrs. Seuthe are going to Japan next year.

15. Mishiko besucht ihre Geschäftsfreunde in München.
Mishiko wird ihre Geschäftsfreunde in München besuchen.

Mishiko is visiting her business associates in Munich.
Mishiko will be visiting her business associates in Munich.

24 Übung 2 / Exercise 2

In this exercise you will repeat and refresh the four most important verb tenses in German. Please insert the missing verb tense:

 Beispiel / Example:

Sprecher:	*Präteritum: Mishiko ging zum Arzt.*
Speaker:	*Simple past: Mishiko went to the doctor.*
Sprecher:	*Perfekt: Mishiko ist zum Arzt gegangen.*
Speaker:	*Perfect: Mishiko went to the doctor.*
Sprecher:	*Präsens: Mishiko geht zum Arzt.*
Speaker:	*Present simple: Mishiko goes to the doctor.*
Sie:	*Futur I: Mishiko wird zum Arzt gehen.*
You:	*Future I: Mishiko will go to the doctor.*
Sprecher:	*Perfekt: Andreas hat sie begleitet.*
Speaker:	*Perfect: Andreas went with her.*
Sprecher:	*Präsens: Andreas begleitet sie.*
Speaker:	*Present simple: Andreas goes with her.*
Sprecher:	*Futur I: Andreas wird sie begleiten.*
Speaker:	*Future I: Andreas will go with her.*
Sie:	*Präteritum: Andreas begleitete sie.*
You:	*Simple past: Andreas went with her.*
Sprecher:	*Präteritum: Mishiko mußte die Tabletten täglich nehmen.*
Speaker:	*Simple past: Mishiko had to take the tablets daily.*
Sprecher:	*Präsens: Mishiko muß die Tabletten täglich nehmen.*
Speaker:	*Present simple: Mishiko has to take the tablets daily.*

| Sprecher | *Futur I: Mishiko wird die Tabletten täglich nehmen müssen.* |
| Speaker: | *Future I: Mishiko will have to take the tablets daily.* |

| Sie: | *Perfekt: Mishiko hat die Tabletten täglich nehmen müssen.* |
| You: | *Perfect: Mishiko had to take the tablets daily.* |

Exercises:

1. Präteritum: Die Sprechstundenhilfe gab Mishiko das Rezept.
Perfekt: Die Sprechstundenhilfe hat Mishiko das Rezept gegeben.
Futur I: Die Sprechstundenhilfe wird Mishiko das Rezept geben.
Präsens: Die Sprechstundenhilfe gibt Mishiko das Rezept.

   Simple past: The receptionist gave Mishiko the prescription.
Perfect: The receptionist gave Mishiko the prescription.
Future I: The receptionist will give Mishiko the prescription.
Simple present: The receptionist gives Mishiko the prescription.

2. Präteritum: Andreas und Mishiko wollten an den Rhein fahren.
Perfekt: Andreas und Mishiko haben an den Rhein fahren wollen.
Präsens: Andreas und Mishiko wollen an den Rhein fahren.
Futur I: Andreas und Mishiko werden an den Rhein fahren wollen.

   Perfect: Andreas and Mishiko wanted to drive along the Rhine.
Perfect: Andreas and Mishiko wanted to drive along the Rhine.
Present simple: Andreas and Mishiko want to drive along the Rhine.
Future I: Andreas and Mishiko will want to drive along the Rhine.

3. Präteritum: Herr Lehmann lud seine Familie zum Essen ein.
Präsens: Herr Lehmann lädt seine Familie zum Essen ein.
Futur I: Herr Lehmann wird seine Familie zum Essen einladen.
Perfekt: Herr Lehmann hat seine Familie zum Essen eingeladen.

   Simple past: Mr. Lehmann invited his family to dinner.
Present simple: Mr. Lehmann invites his family to dinner.
Future I: Mr. Lehmann will invite his family to dinner.
Perfect: Mr. Lehmann invited his family to dinner.

4. Perfekt: Herr und Frau Seuthe haben im Wartezimmer Platz genommen.

Perfect: Mr. and Mrs. Seuthe took seats in the waiting room.

Präsens: Herr und Frau Seuthe nehmen im Wartezimmer Platz.

Present simple: Mr. and Mrs. Seuthe take seats in the waiting room.

Futur I: Herr und Frau Seuthe werden im Wartezimmer Platz nehmen.

Future I: Mr. and Mrs. Seuthe will take seats in the waiting room.

Präteritum: Herr und Frau Seuthe nahmen im Wartezimmer Platz.

Simple past: Mr. and Mrs. Seuthe took seats in the waiting room.

5. Präteritum: Ihr besuchtet eure Freunde.

Simple past: You visited your friends.

Perfekt: Ihr habt eure Freunde besucht.

Perfect: You visited your friends.

Futur I: Ihr werdet eure Freunde besuchen.

Future I: You will visit your friends.

Präsens:Ihr besucht eure Freunde.

Simple present: You visit your friends.

CD4 **Übung 3 / Exercise 3**
TOP5

Please transform the sentences you hear into the imperative!

 Beispiel / Example:

Sprecher: *Mishiko geht zum Arzt.*
Speaker: *Mishiko goes to the doctor.*

Sie: *Geh zum Arzt!*
You: *Go to the doctor!*

Sprecher: *Sie nimmt täglich ihre Tabletten.*
Speaker: *She takes her tablets daily.*

Sie: *Nimm täglich deine Tabletten!*
You: *Take your tablets daily!*

Sprecher: *Herr Lehmann öffnet die Tür.*
Speaker: *Mr. Lehmann opens the door*

Sie: *Öffnen Sie die Tür!*
You: *Open the door!*

Exercice:

1. Mishiko geht zum Arzt.
   Geh zum Arzt!

   Mishiko goes to the doctor.
   Go to the doctor!

2. Sie nimmt täglich ihre Tabletten.
   Nimm täglich deine Tabletten!

   She takes her tablets daily.
   Take your tablets daily!

3. Herr Lehmann öffnet die Tür.
   Öffnen Sie die Tür!

   Mr. Lehmann opens the door
   Open the door!

4. Die Kinder spielen bei dem
   schönen Wetter draußen.
   *Spielt bei dem schönen
   Wetter draußen!*

   The children play outside in the
   nice weather.
   Play outside in the nice weather!

5. Morgen kommt er mich besuchen.
   Komm mich morgen besuchen!

   He will visit me tomorrow.
   Come visit me tomorrow!

6. Sie sprechen wieder mit ihren
   Freunden.
   Sprecht wieder mit euren Freunden!

   They speak again with their friends.
   Go speak again with your friends!

Grammatik / Grammar

1. Das Futur I / *The Future I*

During your stay in Germany you will probably notice quickly that many Germans don't use the Future I in conversation. It is also not necessary, because you can also describe an event in the future by using the present simple tense. In this case, however you must include a temporal phrase to show that you are describing the future.

> **Beispiel:** **Morgen gehe ich zum Arzt.**
> *Example:* *Tomorrow I'm going to the doctor.*

As is so often the case with German, there is again a big difference between the written and spoken language. While you can use simple present in spoken discourse, you should use the Future I when you write.
Please keep in mind Hochdeutsch (High German) grammar rules specify using the Future I. If you want to concentrate primarily on speaking Hochdeutsch, you should use the Future I tense.

The form of the Future I is simple to learn.
Put the conjugated form of the auxiliary verb »werden« at position two in your sentence and put the infinite form of the main verb at the end of the sentence.

> **Beispiel:** **Morgen werde ich zum Arzt gehen.**
> *Exemple:* *Tomorrow I will go to the doctor.*

Here you can read through these example sentences showing the different forms with each personal form:

ich	Morgen werde ich zum Arzt gehen.
du	Morgen wirst du zum Arzt gehen.
er	Morgen wird er zum Arzt gehen.
sie	Morgen wird sie zum Arzt gehen.
es	Morgen wird es zum Arzt gehen.
wir	Morgen werden wir zum Arzt gehen.
ihr	Morgen werdet ihr zum Arzt gehen.
sie/Sie	Morgen werden sie/Sie zum Arzt gehen.

Hinweis / Important informaiton:

Please keep in mind that the Future I is very similar to the passive tense. The only difference is the verb at the end of the sentence.

Passive   *The Participle II is at the end of the sentence.*

Future I   *The Infinitive is at the end of the sentence.*

2. Imperativ / *Imperative*

Along with yes-no questions, imperative sentences are the only sentences where the verb begins the sentence.
Sentences in the imperative always end with an exclamation point.
Of course, you can always include "bitte" (please) in an imperative to make it more polite.

Personal forms:

Singular:	Mach(e) (bitte) deine Hausaufgaben! *Please do your homework!*
Plural:	Macht (bitte) eure Hausaufgaben!
Polite form:	Machen Sie (bitte) Ihre Hausaufgaben!

The polite form can be used both in the singular and plural.
A few verbs change vowels in the imperative (Singular).

Sprechen	Sprich! *(talk!)*
Nehmen	Nimm! *(take!)*
Geben	Gib! *(give!)*
Sehen	Sieh! *(look!)*
Vergessen	Vergiss! *(forget it!)*

3. Genitiv / *Genitive*

The genitive case causes difficulties with masculine and neutral nouns; with feminine nouns the genitive is identical to the dative form.
With masculine and neutral nouns the genitive is mostly formed by adding the suffix "-es". A few words are formed in genitive by only adding "-s".

Nominative	Genitive
das Rezept	des Rezeptes
der Termin	des Termins
der Mann	des Mannes
das Haus	des Hauses

The prepositions *"wegen"* (because) and *"trotz"* (despite) always take genitive.

Example:

> Wegen des schlechten Wetters mußte ich zu Hause bleiben.
> *Because of bad weather, I had to stay home.*

> Trotz des schlechten Wetters mußte ich zu Hause bleiben.
> *Despite the bad weather, I had to stay home.*

The genitive forms are being used less and less. Often the dative is used in place of genitive.
However, when you link two nouns together, you should definitely use the genitive form

> Der Vater meines Vaters ist mein Opa.
> *My father's father is my grandfather.*

Hinweise / Important Information:

The German health insurance system is linked with the national health care systems of most European countries. You can go to any German doctor with your "Internationaler Krankenschein" (international health insurance card), which you can obtain in your own country, without having to pay any additional costs. The health insurance pays for the costs.

For travellers from other countries it is recommended that you join a private health insurance plan before your trip, so that you avoid incurring high health charges.

The network of doctor's surgeries in Germany is widespread. You can safely assume even in rural areas that the nearest doctor is not far.

The same is true for hospitals. You can also receive top quality care there.

In Germany you can only obtain medicine at the chemists. It is forbidden to sell medication in the supermarkets and health stores.

Because there are so many chemists, this limitation should pose no problems at all.

For all medications requiring a prescription, you must go to a doctor to get a prescription. Only with a prescription can you receive these medications.

When you receive a prescription, you must pay a part of the medication cost yourself.

Schriftliche Übung / Written exercises:

Describe the following family relationships:

Beispiel / Example:

Opa / Grandfather:

   Der Vater meines Vaters ist mein Opa.

Übung / Exercises:

   1. Oma:
      Grandmother

   2. Tante:
      Aunt

   3. Onkel:
      Uncle

   4. Neffe:
      Nephew

   5. Cousin:
      Cousin

   6. Schwager:
      Brother-in-law

   7. Urgroßmutter:
      Great-grandmother

Einkaufen gehen

CD4
TOP 6 Going shopping is one of the most important topics of a language course, because every visit to a foreign country deals with this situation. In this lesson you will hear dialogues that show you how to go about purchasing food and clothing.

Wichtige Formulierungen! / Important phrases!
First, listen to these phrases:

Soll ich auf dem Wochenmarkt oder im Supermarkt einkaufen?	Should I go shopping at the weekly market or at the supermarket?
Wo finde ich denn einen Parkplatz?	Where can I park?
Ich hätte gern vier Kalbsschnitzel.	I would like four veal cutlets.
Eine Flasche trockenen Weißwein bitte.	A bottle of dry white wine, please.
Geben Sie mir bitte eine Lage geräucherten Schinken.	I would like a loaf of smoked ham, please.
Ich hätte gern ein Kilo Spinat und drei Pfund Kartoffeln.	I would like one kilo of spinach and three pounds of potatoes, please.
Ich nehme noch ein Stück Schweizer Käse.	I'll take a piece of Swiss cheese, please.
Ich suche einen Pullover für mich.	I am looking for a pullover for myself.
Welche Größe?	Which size is that?
Ich brauche Größe 38.	I am looking for a size 38.
Die Umkleidekabine ist hier.	The changing-room is right here.
Wo finde ich einen Spiegel?	Where can I find a mirror, please?
Der Pullover ist etwas zu groß.	That pullover is somewhat too large.
Ich nehme diesen Pullover.	I'll take this pullover.
Möchte Sie eine Tasche haben?	Would you like a bag?

CD4 TOP 7 Dialog 11 / Dialogue 11

Now listen to the following dialogue:

Mishiko möchte heute Abend ein Essen für Andreas vorbereiten; deshalb möchte sie in die Stadt fahren, um dort einzukaufen.
Mishiko would like to prepare a meal for Andreas for this evening. For this reason, she would like to go shopping in the city.

Mishiko:
Andreas, ich fahre gleich einkaufen, weil ich heute Abend etwas für dich kochen möchte. Wo kann ich am besten Lebensmittel bekommen? Soll ich auf dem Wochenmarkt oder im Supermarkt einkaufen?

Mishiko:
Andreas, I'm going shopping now because I would like to cook something for you tonight. What's the best place to buy groceries? Should I go to the weekly market or to a supermarket?

Andreas:
Frisches Obst und Gemüse kaufst du am Besten auf dem Wochenmarkt. Die anderen Dinge kannst du auch im Supermarkt kaufen.

Andreas:
You can get fresh fruit and vegetables at the weekly market. You will find everything else in the supermarket.

Mishiko:
Gut, dann fahre ich jetzt los. Bis später.

Mishiko:
Good. I am going now. See you later.

Andreas:
Tschüss.

Andreas:
Bye!

Mishiko:
Wo finde ich denn einen Parkplatz?

Mishiko:
Where can I park?

Andreas:
Du parkst am besten im Parkhaus.

Andreas:
I recommend the parking garage.

Mishiko kauft auf dem Wochenmarkt ein.
Mishiko is shopping at the weekly market.

Mishiko:
Guten Tag, ich hätte gern ein Kilo Spinat und drei Pfund Kartoffeln.

Mishiko:
Hello, I would like a kilo of spinach and three pounds of potatoes, please.

Gemüsehändler:
Bitte schön. Darf es sonst noch etwas sein?

Fruit vendor:
Here you are. Would you like anything else?

11 *Dialogue*

Mishiko:
Ja, geben Sie mir bitte noch ein Pfund
weiße Weintrauben.

Mishiko:
Yes, I also would like a pound
of white grapes, please.

Gemüsehändler:
Ist das alles?

Fruit vendor:
Anything else?

Mishiko:
Ja, das ist alles.

Mishiko:
That's all.

Gemüsehändler:
Das macht zusammen 9,97 DM.

Fruit vendor:
Your total is 9.97 DM.

Mishiko:
Bitte. Auf Wiedersehen.

Mishiko:
Thank you. Good bye.

Im Supermarkt kauft Mishiko noch Fleisch und Käse ein.
Mishiko buys some cheese and meat at the supermarket.

Mishiko:
Ich hätte gern vier Kalbsschnitzel und
eine Lage geräucherten Schinken.

Mishiko:
I would like four veal cutlets and a
portion of smoked ham, please.

Verkäuferin:
Hier, bitte. Kann ich noch etwas für
Sie tun?

Saleslady:
Here you are. Can I get anything else
for you?

Mishiko:
Kann ich bei Ihnen auch Käse bekommen?

Mishiko:
Can I also buy cheese here?

Verkäuferin:
Selbstverständlich. Was möchten Sie
denn haben?

Saleslady:
Certainly. What kind would you like?

Mishiko:
Ich nehme noch ein Stück Schweizer
Käse; ungefähr 300 g.

Mishiko:
I'll also take a piece of Swiss cheese,
about 300 grammes.

Verkäuferin:
Bitte.

Saleslady:
Here you are.

Mishiko möchte noch eine Flasche Wein kaufen und geht deshalb zu einem Weinhändler.
Mishiko would also like to buy a bottle of wine, so she goes to a wine merchant.

Mishiko:
Guten Tag. Eine Flasche trockenen
Weißwein bitte.

Mishiko:
Hello. I would like a bottle of dry
white wine, please.

Weinhändler:
Hätten Sie gern französischen,
italienischen oder deutschen Wein?

Wine merchant:
Would you prefer a French,
Italian or German wine?

Mishiko:
Ich möchte einmal deutschen Wein
ausprobieren. Welchen würden Sie
mir denn empfehlen?

Mishiko:
I would like to try a German wine.
What would you recommend?

Weinhändler:
Ich habe hier einen sehr guten Riesling
aus dem Rheingau. Den kann ich Ihnen
wirklich empfehlen.

Wine merchant:
I have a very good Riesling
from the Rhine Valley. I can
strongly recommend it.

Mishiko:
Gut, dann nehme ich diese Flasche.

Mishiko:
Good, then I'll take this bottle.

Mishiko möchte sich noch einen neuen Pullover kaufen und geht in eine Boutique.
Mishiko would also like to buy a pullover, so she goes to a boutique.

Mishiko:
Ich suche einen Pullover für mich.

Mishiko:
I'm looking for a pullover for myself.

Verkäuferin:
Welche Größe?

Saleslady:
Which size?

Mishiko:
Ich brauche Größe 38.

Mishiko:
I take a size 38.

Verkäuferin:
Da kann ich Ihnen diese Pullover zeigen.

Saleslady:
Here, I can show you these pullovers.

Mishiko:
Dieser gefällt mir sehr gut. Wo finde
ich denn eine Umkleidekabine?

Mishiko:
I like this one very much. Where are
the changing-rooms?

Verkäuferin:
Die Umkleidekabine ist hier.

Saleslady:
The changing-room is over here.

Mishiko:
Der Pullover ist etwas zu groß; haben
Sie den gleichen auch in Größe 36?

Mishiko:
This pullover is a bit too large —
do you have the same in size 36?

Verkäuferin:
Ja, hier.

Saleslady:
Yes, here you are.

Mishiko:
Ich nehme diesen Pullover.

Verkäuferin:
Danke. Möchten Sie eine Tasche haben?

Mishiko:
Ja bitte. Auf Wiedersehen.

Mishiko:
I'll take this pullover.

Saleslady:
Thank you. Would you like a bag with that?

Mishiko:
Yes, please. Good bye.

I recommend that you listen to the entire dialogue one more time. You should also repeat the individual sentences so that you can get the right feel for the correct pronunciation.
(If the dialogue is too fast, please use the pause button on your CD player.)

D4 Übung 1 / Exercise 1
P8

Now put the sentences you hear into indirect speech:

B **Beispiel / Example:**

Sprecher:	*Mishiko sagt: "Ich gehe heute Morgen einkaufen."*
Speaker:	*Mishiko says "I'm going shopping this morning."*
Sie:	*Mishiko sagt, dass sie heute Morgen einkaufen gehe.*
You:	*Mishiko says that she is going shopping this morning.*
Sprecher:	*Andreas sagt zu Mishiko: "Du parkst am besten im Parkhaus."*
Speaker:	*Andreas says to Mishiko, "You should park at the parking garage".*
Sie:	*Andreas sagt, dass Mishiko am besten im Parkhaus parke.*
You.	*Andreas says to Mishiko that she should park at the parking garage.*
Sprecher:	*Herr Seuthe sagte zu Andreas: "Sie fahren besser mit der Bahn."*
Speaker:	*Mr. Seuthe says to Andreas, "You should take the train".*
Sie:	*Herr Seuthe sagte, dass Andreas besser mit der Bahn fahre.*
You:	*Mr. Seuthe says that Andreas should take the train.*

 Exercice:

1. Die Frau antwortete: "Ich werde Herrn Lehmann am Dienstag besuchen."
   Die Frau antwortete, dass sie Herrn Lehmann am Dienstag besuchen werde.

   The woman answered, "I will visit Mr. Lehmann on Tuesday."
   The woman said that she would visit Mr. Lehmann on Tuesday.

2. Die Kinder sagten: "Wir gehen gleich auf den Spielplatz."
   Die Kinder sagten, dass sie gleich auf den Spielplatz gingen.

   The children said, "We are going to the playground now."
   The children said that they were going to the playground now.

3. Mishiko sagte zu der Verkäuferin: "Ich brauche Größe 38." *Mishiko sagte zu der Verkäuferin, dass sie Größe 38 brauche.*

Mishiko said to the saleslady, "I take a size 38.". *Mishiko said to the saleslady that she took a size 38.*

4. Mishiko sagt zu Andreas: "Ich habe mir heute einen neuen Pullover gekauft." *Mishiko sagt zu Andreas, dass sie sich heute einen neuen Pullover gekauft habe.*

Mishiko told Andreas, "I bought a new pullover today." *Mishiko told Andreas that she bought a new pullover today.*

5. Herr und Frau Seuthe sagten: "Gestern waren wir im Schauspielhaus." *Herr und Frau Seuthe sagten, dass sie gestern im Schauspielhaus gewesen seien.*

Mr. and Mrs. Seuthe said, "We went to the theatre yesterday." *Mr. and Mrs. Seuthe said that they went to the theatre yesterday.*

6. Mishiko sagt am Telefon: "Ich bin gerade in Köln." *Mishiko sagt am Telefon, dass sie gerade in Köln sei.*

On the phone, Mishiko says "I am already in Cologne." *On the phone, Mishiko says that she would be in Cologne now.*

7. Herr und Frau Seuthe sagen zu Mishiko: "Wir fahren Sie mit dem Auto nach Hause." *Herr und Frau Seuthe sagen zu Mishiko, dass sie sie mit dem Auto nach Hause führen.*

Mr. and Mrs. Seuthe tell Mishiko "We'll drive you back home." *Mr. and Mrs. Seuthe tell Mishiko that they would drive her back home.*

8. Die Kinder sagen zu der Mutter: "Wir machen gerade unsere Hausaufgaben." *Die Kinder sagen zu der Mutter, dass sie gerade ihre Hausaufgaben machen würden.*

The children tell their mother, "We are starting our homework now." *The children tell their mother that they are starting their homework now.*

9. Andreas sagte zu seinen Freunden: "Ihr seid alle zu meinem Geburtstag eingeladen." *Andreas sagte zu seinen Freunden, dass sie alle zu seinem Geburtstag eingeladen seien.*

Andreas told his friends, "You are all invited to my birthday party". *Andreas told his friends they were all invited to his birthday party.*

13. Sie versprachen ihm: "Wir werden dich bestimmt besuchen." *Sie versprachen ihm, daß sie ihn bestimmt besuchen würden.*

They promised him, "We'll definitely come by." *They promised him that they would definitely come by.*

CD4 Übung 2 / Exercise 2
TOP 9

Please transform the sentences you hear into an infinitive sentence with "zu"!

B Beispiel / Example:

Sprecher: *Ich glaube, dass ich heute Zeit habe.*
Speaker: *I think I that have time today.*

Sie: *Ich glaube, heute Zeit zu haben.*
You: *I think I have time today.*

Sprecher: *Mishiko hofft, dass sie einen Parkplatz findet.*
Speaker: *Mishiko hopes that she can find a parking space.*

Sie: *Mishiko hofft, einen Parkplatz zu finden.*
You: *Mishiko hopes to find a parking space.*

Sprecher: *Wir hoffen, dass wir euch heute Nachmittag treffen.*
Speaker: *We hope that we will see you this afternoon.*

Sie: *Wir hoffen, euch heute Nachmittag zu treffen.*
You: *We hope to see you this afternoon.*

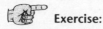 Exercise:

1. Mishiko verspricht, dass sie bald wieder nach Deutschland kommt.
Mishiko verspricht, bald wieder nach Deutschland zu kommen.

   Mishiko promises that she will come back to Germany soon.
Mishiko promises to come back to Germany soon.

2. Ich glaube, dass ich heute Zeit habe.
Ich glaube, heute Zeit zu haben.

   I think I that have time today.

   I think I have time today.

3. Mishiko hofft, dass sie einen Parkplatz findet.
Mishiko hofft, einen Parkplatz zu finden.

   Mishiko hopes that she can find a parking space.
Mishiko hopes to find a parking space.

4. Wir hoffen, dass wir euch heute Nachmittag treffen.
   Wir hoffen, euch heute Nachmittag zu treffen.

We hope that we will see you this afternoon.
We hope to see you this afternoon.

5. Mishiko glaubt, dass sie Größe 38 hat.
   Mishiko glaubt, Größe 38 zu haben.

Mishiko thinks that she takes a size 38.
Mishiko thinks she takes a size 38.

6. Andreas versprach, dass er alle seine Freunde einlädt.
   Andreas versprach, alle seine Freunde einzuladen.

Andreas promised that he would invite all his friends.
Andreas promised to invite all his friends.

7. Herr und Frau Seuthe haben geglaubt, dass sie ihren Koffer vergessen haben.
   Herr und Frau Seuthe haben geglaubt, ihren Koffer vergessen zu haben.

Mr. and Mrs. Seuthe believed that they had forgotten their suitcases.
Mr. and Mrs. Seuthe believed they had forgotten their suitcase.

8. Der Autofahrer glaubte, dass er nicht zu schnell fuhr.
   Der Autofahrer glaubte, nicht zu schnell gefahren zu sein.

The driver believed that he was not driving too fast.
The driver believed he was not driving too fast.

9. Das Kind versprach, daß es so etwas nicht wieder tut.
   Das Kind versprach, so etwas nicht wieder zu tun.

The child promised that he would not do it again.
The child promised never to do it again.

10. Mishiko hat Andreas versprochen, daß sie heute Abend kocht.
    Mishiko hat Andreas versprochen, heute Abend zu kochen.

Mishiko promised Andreas that she would cook this evening.
Mishiko promised Andreas she would cook this evening.

Grammatik / Grammar

Konjunktiv I / Subjunctive I

When you want to use indirect speech in German, you must use the *subjunctive I*. With the *subjunctive I* you can express the idea that you are only repeating the speech of someone else without guaranteeing that the statement is completely true.

As with the *subjunctive II* you can also mix this with other tenses of the verb.

To form the subjunctive I, you must attach an "-e" suffix to the root of the verb in the present simple.

machen - make

Personalform Personal form	Präsens Present	Konjunktiv I Subjunctive 1
ich	mache	mache
du	machst	machest
er	macht	mache
sie	macht	mache
es	macht	mache
wir	machen	machen
ihr	macht	machet
sie/Sie	machen	machen

As you can see, a few of the cases of subjunctive I are identical to the simple present. Whenever this problem occurs, you must use the subjunctive II. If, as a result, this creates a possible confusion with an identical simple past verb form, then you should use the form with "würde" instead.

Example:

Er sagt: " Wir machen bestimmt einen Einkauf."
He says "We will definitely make a purchase".

Er sagt, dass sie bestimmt einen Einkauf machen.
He says that they will definitely make a purchase.

Because the verb *"machen"* in Subjunctive I is no different from the form of the verb in simple present, the **Subjunctive II** has to be used instead.

Er sagt, dass sie bestimmt einen Einkauf machten.

The verb *"machen"* is one of the weak verbs, and for this reason there is no difference between **Subjunctive II** and simple past. In this case the form with *"würde"* should be used.

Er sagt, dass sie bestimmt einen Einkauf machen würden.

Now look at the conjugation of the auxiliary verbs "haben" and "sein":

Personalform Personal form	Präsens Present	Konjunktiv I Subjunctive 1
ich	habe/bin	habe/sei
du	hast/bist	habest/seist
er	hat/ist	habe/sei
sie	hat/ist	habe/sei
es	hat/ist	habe/sei
wir	haben/sind	haben/seien
ihr	habt/seid	habet/seiet
sie/Sie	haben/sind	haben/seien

In general indirect speech should be formed with a **"dass-Satz"** ("that-sentence"). However, you can also use the following form:

> Er sagt, dass er keine Zeit habe.
> *He says that he has no time.*

> Er sagt, er habe keine Zeit.
> *He says he has no time.*

Both forms have the same meaning.

Infinitiv mit *"zu"* / Infinitive with *"zu"*

You have probably already noticed that sentences with the conjunction *"dass"* (that) occur quite frequently in German. In order to avoid sounding too monotonous, there is the possibility to use an infinitive phrase with *"zu"* instead of *"dass"*.
However, you can only use this form when the subject of the main clause is the same as the subject of the dependent clause with *"dass"*.

Example:

> Andreas glaubt, dass er heute Abend Zeit hat.
> *Andreas believes that he has time tonight.*

The subject *"Andreas"* is the same as the subject "er" in the dependent clause with "dass". For this reason you can also use the following form:

> Andreas glaubt, heute Abend Zeit zu haben.

Because infinitive clauses are also dependent clauses, it is very important that you put the verb (in this case the infinitive) at the end of the sentence.

Hinweise / Important information:

As in most European countries you also have the possibility in Germany to go shopping without having to speak. You only need visit the countless supermarkets where you just put the goods in your shopping basket.
This is certainly a practical way to shop.
You can however obtain many food items that are much fresher and in greater variety at the weekly markets. Here you also have the possibility to practice your knowledge of German.
There are a few important sentence forms that you can use to express what you want when you shop.

Ich hätte gern ...	*I would like...*
Ich möchte gern ...	*I would like...*
Geben Sie mir bitte ...	*Could you give me...., please?*

The verbs *"hätte"* and *"möchte"* are in the **subjunctive II** because it makes the sentence more polite. Certainly your wishes are not unreal situations. These forms have become standard over the course of time and you should use them accordingly.
When you express your wishes with *"Geben Sie mir bitte ..."*, be sure not to forget to include the word *"bitte"* (please). This is an imperative, or command, and it sounds very impolite when you address a sales clerk like this, without including *"bitte"*.

Schriftliche Übung / Written exercises:

Insert the subjunctive I in the following:

1. Andreas hat gesagt, dass er morgen nach München _____. (fahren)

2. Mishiko verspricht, dass sie bald wieder nach Deutschland _____. (kommen)

3. Herr und Frau Seuthe sagten, dass sie in diesem Jahr nach Italien _____. (fahren)

4. Herr Lehmann behauptete, dass er schon in Berlin gewesen _____. (sein)

5. Ihr habt gesagt, dass ihr eure Arbeit schon lange gemacht _____. (haben)

6. Ich habe nicht versprochen, dass ich euch noch in diesem Monat _____. (besuchen)

7. Wir sagten euch schon gestern, dass wir die Getränke _____. (mitbringen)

8. Sie antwortete, dass sie heute unmöglich kommen _____. (können)

9. Andreas sagte, dass Mishiko bald wieder nach Japan fliegen _____. (müssen)

10. Ich sagte, dass ich vorige Woche schon in München gewesen _____. (sein)

Feste und Traditionen

CD4
TOP10
Now you will learn the most important holidays in Germany! You will also learn how people celebrate in Germany and what traditions exist in this country.

Wichtige Formulierungen! / Important phrases!
First, listen to these phrases:

Weihnachten ist am 25. und 26. Dezember.	Christmas is on the 25th and 26th of December.
Wann ist Ostern?	When is Easter?
Ostern ist immer im Frühling.	Easter is always in Spring.
Welche Feiertage gibt es in Deutschland?	What holidays do you observe in Germany?
Wie wird bei euch Geburtstag gefeiert?	How do you celebrate birthdays in your country?
Wo wird überall Karneval gefeiert?	Where is Carnival celebrated?
Feiert man Karneval in allen Gegenden gleich?	Is Carnival celebrated the same way in all regions?
Du musst dir einen Rosenmontagszug ansehen!	You must see the parade on Rosenmontag!
Was ist ein Jahrmarkt?	What is an Annual market?
Ist Kirmes und Jahrmarkt das Gleiche?	Are Kirmes and Annual market the same thing?
Wird das Oktoberfest nur in München gefeiert?	Is Oktoberfest only celebrated in Munich?
In vielen Städten gibt es Schützenfeste.	In many cities there are shooting festivals and fairs.

CD4 Dialog 12 / Dialogue 12

Now listen to the following dialogue:

Mishiko und Andreas sitzen zusammen. Mishiko möchte gern von Andreas etwas über die Feste und Feierlichkeiten in Deutschland erfahren.
Mishiko and Andreas are sitting together. Mishiko would like to learn something about the festivals and holidays in Germany from Andreas.

Mishiko:
Ich habe schon sehr viel über Deutschland erfahren. Ich weiß aber fast nichts über eure Feiertage. Erzähle mir bitte etwas darüber!

Mishiko:
I already have learned a lot about Germany, but I hardly know anything about your holidays. Please tell me something about that!

Andreas:
Das ist nicht einfach; aber ich möchte es versuchen. Ich werde mit dem Weihnachtsfest beginnen.

Andreas:
It's not easy, but I'll try. I will start with Christmas.

Mishiko:
Wann wird Weihnachten gefeiert?

Mishiko:
When is Christmas celebrated?

Andreas:
Weihnachten ist am 25. und 26. Dezember. Beide Tage sind Feiertage und die Menschen müssen nicht arbeiten. Der 24. Dezember wird auch "Heiligabend" genannt. In vielen Familien wird an diesem Tag beschert.

Andreas:
Christmas is on the 25th and 26th of December. Both days are holidays and people don't work on those days. The 24th of December is also called "Heiligabend". Many families exchange presents on this day.

Mishiko:
Was bedeutet "beschert"?

Mishiko:
What does "beschert" mean?

Andreas:
Das bedeutet, dass es an diesem Tag die Geschenke gibt. Sie werden meistens unter den Tannenbaum gelegt.

Andreas:
It means that on this day presents are exchanged. Most are put under the Christmas tree.

Mishiko:
Ist Ostern auch immer an zwei festen Tagen?

Mishiko:
Is Easter also celebrated on two definite days?

Andreas:
Nein, es gibt immer einen Ostersonntag
und einen Ostermontag. Ostern ist
immer im Frühling.

Andreas:
No, but there is always an Easter Sunday and
an Easter Monday. Easter is always
in Spring.

Mishiko:
Welche Feiertage gibt es noch
in Deutschland?

Mishiko:
What other holidays are there
in Germany?

Andreas:
Das kann ich nicht so genau sagen.
Jedes Bundesland hat eine eigene
Regelung. Es kommt darauf an, ob ein
Bundesland mehr evangelisch oder
katholisch ist.

Andreas:
I can't say for sure. Each state has its own
rules. It all depends if a state is more
Protestant or Catholic.

Mishiko:
Aber du kannst mir bestimmt erzählen,
wie in Deutschland Geburtstag
gefeiert wird.

Mishiko:
But you can definitely tell me
how birthdays are celebrated
in Germany.

Andreas:
Das ist noch schwieriger. In jeder
Familie gibt es eine eigene Tradition,
wie sie ihre Geburtstage feiern.

Andreas:
That's even harder. Every family
has its own traditions for
celebrating birthdays.

Mishiko:
Ich habe auch gehört, dass es bei euch
eine "fünfte Jahreszeit" gibt. Kannst du
mir erklären, was das ist? Ich kenne
nämlich nur den Frühling, den Sommer,
den Herbst und den Winter.

Mishiko:
I've also heard that there is a fifth season.
Can you explain what that is. I only know
of Spring, Summer, Autumn and Winter.

Andreas:
Als "fünfte Jahreszeit" wird der
Karneval bezeichnet.

Andreas:
The "fifth season" is Carnival.

Mishiko:
Wo wird überall Karneval gefeiert?

Mishiko:
Where is Carnival celebrated?

Andreas:
In vielen Gegenden Deutschlands wird
Karneval gefeiert. In Süddeutschland
nennt man es aber nicht Karneval
sondern "Fasching".

Andreas:
Carnival is celebrated in many regions of
Germany. In South Germany they don't call it
Carnival, but rather "Fasching".

Mishiko:
Gehört der "Rosenmontag" auch zum Karneval?

Mishiko:
Is "Rosenmontag" a part of carnival?

Andreas:
Ja, der "Rosenmontag" ist der wichtigste Tag des Karnevals. An diesem Tag gehen die Menschen in Kostümen auf die Straße; auch die Karnevalszüge finden an diesem Tag statt. Du musst dir einen Rosenmontagszug ansehen.

Andreas:
Yes, "Rosenmontag" is the most important day of carnival. On this day the people wear costumes on the street, and there are also many parades on this day. You must see the parade on Rosenmontag.

Mishiko:
Gerne, wenn ich das nächste Mal in Deutschland bin. Was ist denn ein Jahrmarkt? Ich weiß nur, was ein Wochenmarkt ist. Kannst du mir den Unterschied erklären?

Mishiko:
I would like to, maybe when I visit Germany next time. What is an Annual market? I only know what a weekly market is. Can you explain the difference to me?

Andreas:
Der Wochenmarkt ist ein ganz normaler Markt, auf dem du einkaufen kannst. Es heißt Wochenmarkt, weil er einmal pro Woche stattfindet. Ein Jahrmarkt findet aber nur einmal im Jahr statt. In vielen Gegenden Deutschland nennt man einen Jahrmarkt auch Kirmes.

Andreas:
The weekly market is a normal market where you can shop. It's called a weekly market because it happens once a week. An Annual market only takes place once a year. In many regions they also call annual markets "Kirmes".

Mishiko:
Jetzt musst du mir aber noch erklären, was eine Kirmes ist.

Mishiko:
Now you must explain what "Kirmes" is.

Andreas:
Entschuldigung. Eine Kirmes ist ein Fest, das in vielen Städten gefeiert wird. Dort kannst du trinken, essen und mit dem Karussell fahren. Junge und alte Menschen treffen sich auf dem Jahrmarkt oder auf der Kirmes.

Andreas:
Sorry. "Kirmes" is a festival celebrated in many cities. You can drink, eat and ride the carousels. People of all ages meet up at the Annual market or Kirmes.

Mishiko:
Ist das Oktoberfest in München auch ein Jahrmarkt?

Mishiko:
Is the Oktoberfest in Munich also an Annual market?

Andreas:
Ja, das ist der größte Jahrmarkt in Deutschland.

Andreas:
Yes, it is the largest Annual market in all of Germany.

Mishiko:
Wird das Oktoberfest nur in München
gefeiert, oder gibt es das auch in
anderen Städten?

Mishiko:
Is Oktoberfest only celebrated in Munich
or also in other cities?

Andreas:
Oktoberfeste gibt es auch in anderen
Städten, aber das Oktoberfest in
München ist das bekannteste.

Andreas:
There are Oktoberfests in other
cities, but the Oktoberfest in
Munich is the most famous.

Mishiko:
Jetzt möchte ich nur noch wissen,
was ein Schützenfest ist?

Mishiko:
Now I would like to know
what a shooting festival is.

Andreas:
Das Oktoberfest ist eigentlich auch
ein Schützenfest. Mehrere Vereine aus
einer Stadt veranstalten zusammen
eine Kirmes. Diese Kirmes wird dann
Schützenfest genannt.

Andreas:
Actually, Oktoberfest is also a
shooting festival. Many clubs from
one city get together and organise
a Kirmes. This is then called
a shooting festival.

Mishiko:
Danke. Du hast mir alles sehr gut erklärt.

Mishiko:
Thank you. You've explained everything
very well.

Andreas:
Bitte. Gern geschehen.

Andreas:
You're welcome. Glad to do it.

**I recommend that you listen to the entire dialogue one more time. You should
also repeat the individual sentences so that you can get the right feel for the
correct pronunciation.
(If the dialogue is too fast, please use the pause button on your CD player.)**

CD4 TOP12 Übung 1 / Exercise 1

From two main clauses you hear, please create a main and dependent clause: Please use the conjunctions you hear.

B **Beispiel / Example:**

Sprecher: *Andreas ist nach Köln gefahren.*
Speaker: *Andreas drove to Cologne.*
Sprecher: *Andreas fuhr nach München.*
Speaker: *Andreas drove to Munich.*

bevor
before

○ 1.
○ 2.
○ 3.

Sie: *Bevor Andreas nach Köln gefahren ist,*
fuhr er nach München.
You: *Before Andreas drove to Cologne,*
he drove to Munich.

Sprecher: *Andreas erklärt Mishiko die deutschen Feiertage.*
Speaker: *Andreas explains German holidays to Mishiko.*

Sprecher: *Mishiko hört ihm zu.*
Speaker: *Mishiko listens to him.*

während
while

Sie: *Während Andreas Mishiko die deutschen Feiertage erklärt, hört*
sie zu.
You: *While Andreas explains the German holidays to Mishiko,*
she listens.

Sprecher: *Mishiko kennt das Oktoberfest in München.*
You: *Mishiko knows about the Oktoberfest in Munich.*

Sprecher: *Es ist das bekannteste.*
You: *It is the most famous one.*

weil
because

Sie: *Mishiko kennt das Oktoberfest in München, weil es das*
bekannteste ist.
You: *Mishiko knows about the Oktoberfest in Munich because it is*
the most famous.

Exercise:

1. Andreas ist nach Köln gefahren.
Andreas fuhr nach München.
bevor
***Bevor Andreas nach Köln gefahren
ist, fuhr er nach München.***

   Andreas drove to Cologne.
Andreas drove to Munich.
before
***Before Andreas drove to Cologne,
he drove to Munich.***

2. Andreas erklärt Mishiko die
deutschen Feiertage.
Mishiko hört ihm zu.
während
***Während Andreas Mishiko die
deutschen Feiertage erklärt,
hört sie zu.***

   Andreas explains German holidays
to Mishiko.
Mishiko listens to him.
while
***While Andreas explains the German
holidays to Mishiko, she listens.***

3. Mishiko kennt das Oktoberfest
in München.
Es ist das bekannteste.
weil
***Mishiko kennt das Oktoberfest
in München, weil es das
bekannteste ist.***

   Mishiko knows about the Oktoberfest
in Munich.
Es ist das bekannteste.
because
***Mishiko knows about the Oktoberfest
in Munich because it is the
most famous.***

4. Andreas glaubt.
Das Wetter wird besser.
dass
***Andreas glaubt, dass das Wetter
besser wird.***

   Andreas believes.
The weather will improve.
That
***Andreas believes that the weather
will improve.***

5. Herr Seuthe wartet auf seine Frau.
Sie kann sich noch den Mantel
anziehen.
damit
***Herr Seuthe wartet auf seine Frau,
damit sie sich noch den Mantel
anziehen kann.***

   Mr. Seuthe waits for his wife.
She can put on her overcoat.
so that
***Mr. Seuthe waits for his wife,
so that she can put on
her overcoat.***

6. Mishiko geht heute Nachmittag einkaufen.

    Mishiko is going shopping this afternoon.

    Sie hat eigentlich keine Zeit.

    She really doesn't have time.

    obwohl

    although

    Mishiko geht heute Nachmittag einkaufen, obwohl sie eigentlich keine Zeit hat.

    Mishiko is going shopping this afternoon, although she really doesn't have time.

7. Andreas beantwortete Mishikos Frage.

    Andreas answered Mishiko's questions.

    Er erklärte ihr den Rosenmontag.

    He explained Rosenmontag to her.

    indem

    in that

    Andreas beantwortete Mishikos Frage, indem er ihr den Rosenmontag erklärte.

    Andreas answered Mishiko's questions, in that he explained Rosenmontag to her.

8. Ich komme dich morgen Abend besuchen.

    Ich komme dich morgen Abend besuchen.

    Ich habe Zeit.

    I have time.

    wenn

    if

    Ich komme dich morgen Abend besuchen, wenn ich Zeit habe.

    I will visit you tomorrow evening, if I have time.

9. Mishiko will sich bei Andreas melden.

    Mishiko wants to contact Andreas.

    Sie ist in Deutschland.

    She is in Germany.

    sobald

    as soon as

    Mishiko will sich bei Andreas melden, sobald sie in Deutschland ist.

    Mishiko wants to contact Andreas as soon as she is in Germany.

10. Andreas hat Mishiko sehr geholfen.

    Andreas helped Mishiko a lot.

    Er hat es nicht gewusst.

    He didn't actually know it.

    ohne dass

    without

    Andreas hat Mishiko sehr geholfen, ohne dass er es gewusst hat.

    Andreas helped Mishiko a lot without actually knowing it.

Übung 2 / Exercise 2

Create relative clauses from the statements you hear:

B Beispiel / Example:

Sprecher: *Das Auto steht auf dem Parkplatz.*
Es ist rot.
Speaker: *The car is in the parking space.*
It is red.

Sie: *Das Auto, das rot ist, steht auf dem*
Parkplatz.
You: *The car that is red is in the*
parking space.

Sprecher: *Mishiko fliegt zurück nach Japan.*
Ich kenne sie schon seit fünf Jahren.
Speaker: *Mishiko is flying back to Japan.*
I have known her for five years.

Sie: *Mishiko, die ich schon seit fünf Jahren kenne, fliegt zurück*
nach Japan.
You: *Mishiko, who I have known for five years, is flying back to Japan.*

Sprecher: *Der Junge feiert heute seinen Geburtstag.*
Ich bin sein Onkel.
Speaker: *The boy is celebrating his birthday today.*
I am his uncle.

Sie: *Der Junge, dessen Onkel ich bin, feiert heute seinen*
Geburtstag.
You: *The boy, whose uncle I am, is celebrating*
his birthday today.

 **Exercise:**

1. Dort steht mein Freund.　That is my friend, over there.
Ich bin mit ihm in Urlaub gefahren.　I went on holiday with him.
Dort steht mein Freund, mit dem　*That is my friend, with whom*
ich in Urlaub gefahren bin.　*I went on holiday.*

5. Mishiko freut sich auf das　Mishiko is looking forward to
Weihnachtsfest in Deutschland.　Christmas in Germany.
Es wird am 25. Dezember gefeiert.　It will be celebrated on the 25th
　of December.

Mishiko freut sich auf das　*Mishiko is looking forward to Christmas*
Weihnachtsfest in Deutschland,　*in Germany, which will be celebrated*
das am 25. Dezember gefeiert wird.　*on the 25th of December.*

6. Das Kind schenkt der alten　The child is giving the old lady
Frau ein Buch zu Weihnachten.　a book for Christmas.
Sie kennt es hoffentlich noch nicht.　Hopefully, she has not read it yet.

Das Kind schenkt der alten Frau　*For Christmas, the child is giving*
ein Buch, das sie hoffentlich　*the old lady a book that, hopefully,*
noch nicht kennt, zu Weihnachten.　*she has not yet read.*

7. Das Oktoberfest in München　The Oktoberfest in Munich
ist sehr bekannt.　is very famous.
Auf ihm wird viel Bier getrunken.　At it, much beer is consumed.

Das Oktoberfest in München,　*The Oktoberfest in Munich,*
auf dem viel Bier getrunken　*where much beer is consumed,*
wird, ist sehr bekannt.　*is very famous.*

8. Ich schenke der Frau　I am sending the woman
einen Strauß Blumen.　a bouquet of flowers.
Ich bin ihr Ehemann.　I am her husband
Ich schenke der Frau, deren　*I am sending the woman, who is my wife,*
Ehemann ich bin, einen　*a bouquet of flowers.*
Strauß Blumen.

9. Der Garten wurde neu angelegt.　The garden was newly re-planted.
In ihm wachsen viele　Many pretty flowers are growing.
schöne Blumen.
Der Garten, in dem viele schöne　*The garden where many pretty*
Blumen wachsen, wurde　*flowers are growing was newly*
neu angelegt.　*re-planted.*

10. Das Flugzeug kam pünktlich auf dem Kölner Flughafen an. In ihm saß Mishiko. *Das Flugzeug, in dem Mishiko saß, kam pünktlich auf dem Kölner Flughafen an.*

The plane arrived at Cologne Airport on time. Mishiko was on the flight. *The plane which Mishiko was on arrived at Cologne Airport on time.*

GRAMMATIK / GRAMMAR

Nebensätze / Dependent clauses

In the German language there is a very important difference between a main clause and a dependent clause:
The position of the verb.
Always keep in mind that in a main clause the conjugated verb always takes the second position in the clause.
In a dependent clause the conjugated verb always takes the last position.
As long as you keep these rules in mind, you will avoid making many mistakes with dependent clauses.

Example:

Hauptsatz *main clause:*	Es **regnet** sehr stark. *It is raining hard.*
Nebensatz *dependent clause:*	..., weil es stark **regnet**. *because it is raining hard.*
Hauptsatz *main clause:*	Es **hat** stark geregnet. *It rained hard.*
Nebensatz *dependent clause:*	..., weil es stark geregnet **hat**. *...because it rained hard.*
Hauptsatz *main clause:*	Das Kind **wollte** nicht zur Schule gehen. *The child didn't want to go to school.*
Nebensatz *dependent clause:*	..., weil das Kind nicht zur Schule gehen **wollte**. *...because the child didn't want to go to school.*

Relativsätze / Relative clauses

Relative clauses are also dependent clauses. Every rule that is valid for dependent clauses is also true for relative clauses. The difference between the two clause types is that relative clauses always add extra details about a noun.
It is an advantage if you always place the relative clause after the noun it modifies. There are other possibilities, but these make the sentence much more difficult to understand.
Relative clauses can also begin with a preposition.

Examples:

Der Mann, den ich kenne, hat sich ein neues Auto gekauft.
The man I know bought a new car.

Der Parkplatz, auf dem viele Autos stehen, wurde neu gebaut.
The parking garage, in which many cars are parked, was built recently.

Hinweise / Important Information

During your stay in Germany, if you have the possibility to visit one of the big festivals, you should definitely take the opportunity to do so.
From the many festivals that take place over all of Germany, I would like to recommend two in particular:

der rheinische Karneval
(The Rhine-area Carnival)

das Oktoberfest in München
(Oktoberfest in Munich)

The Rhine-area Carnival takes place primarily in the cities of Düsseldorf, Cologne, Bonn und Mainz.
Of course there are many other large and attractive festivals in other cities and regions that are every bit as impressive as the biggest and most famous ones.
When you come to Germany, you should definitely look for information about whether the region you plan to visit also has one of these festivals.

Schriftliche Übung: / Written exercises

Explain the following composite nouns by creating relative clauses:

1. Parkplatz (parking garage)

   Ein Parkplatz ist ein Gelände, _____

   _____

2. Hochhaus (sky scraper)

   Ein Hochhaus ist ein Gebäude, _____

   _____

3. Farbfernseher (colour TV)

   Ein Farbfernseher ist ein Gerät, _____

   _____

4. Flussschiff (riverboat)

   Ein Flussschiff ist ein Fahrzeug, _____

   _____

5. Videorecorder (videorecorder)

   Ein Videorecorder ist ein Gerät, _____

   _____

CD4 Listen now to the most common irregular verbs:
TOP14

Infinitive	Past	Participle II	Subjunctive II
beginnen	begann	begonnen	begönne
beißen	biss	gebissen	bisse
biegen	bog	gebogen	böge
bieten	bot	geboten	böte
binden	band	gebunden	bände
bitten	bat	gebeten	bäte
bleiben	blieb	geblieben	bliebe
braten	briet	gebraten	briete
brechen	brach	gebrochen	bräche
erlöschen	erlosch	erloschen	erlösche
essen	aß	gegessen	äße
fahren	fuhr	gefahren	führe
fallen	fiel	gefallen	fiele
fangen	fing	gefangen	finge
finden	fand	gefunden	fände
fliegen	flog	geflogen	flöge
fließen	floss	geflossen	flösse
frieren	fror	gefroren	fröre
geben	gab	gegeben	gäbe
gehen	ging	gegangen	ginge
geschehen	geschah	geschehen	geschähe
gewinnen	gewann	gewonnen	gewänne
hängen	hing	gehangen	hinge
heben	hob	gehoben	höbe
heißen	hieß	geheißen	hieße
helfen	half	geholfen	hülfe
klingen	klang	geklungen	klänge
kommen	kam	gekommen	käme
lassen	ließ	gelassen	ließe
laufen	lief	gelaufen	liefe

Infinitive	Past	Participle II	Subjunctive II
leihen	lieh	geliehen	liehe
lesen	las	gelesen	läse
liegen	lag	gelegen	läge
lügen	log	gelogen	löge
nehmen	nahm	genommen	nähme
raten	riet	geraten	riete
reiben	rieb	gerieben	riebe
reißen	riss	gerissen	risse
reiten	ritt	geritten	ritte
riechen	roch	gerochen	röche
rufen	rief	gerufen	riefe
scheinen	schien	geschienen	schiene
schieben	schob	geschoben	schöbe
schießen	schoss	geschossen	schösse
schlafen	schlief	geschlafen	schliefe
schlagen	schlug	geschlagen	schlüge
schließen	schloss	geschlossen	schlösse
schmeißen	schmiss	geschmissen	schmisse
schneiden	schnitt	geschnitten	schnitte
schreiben	schrieb	geschrieben	schriebe
schreien	schrie	geschrien	schrie
schreiten	schritt	geschritten	schritte
schweigen	schwieg	geschwiegen	schwiege
schwimmen	schwamm	geschwommen	schwämme
sehen	sah	gesehen	sähe
singen	sang	gesungen	sänge
sinken	sank	gesunken	sänke
sprechen	sprach	gesprochen	spräche
springen	sprang	gesprungen	spränge
stehen	stand	gestanden	stünde
stehlen	stahl	gestohlen	stähle

Infinitive	Past	Participle II	Subjunctive II
sterben	starb	gestorben	stürbe
stoßen	stieß	gestoßen	stieße
streiten	stritt	gestritten	stritte
tragen	trug	getragen	trüge
treffen	traf	getroffen	träfe
treten	trat	getreten	träte
trinken	trank	getrunken	tränke
vergessen	vergaß	vergessen	vergäße
verlieren	verlor	verloren	verlöre
waschen	wusch	gewaschen	wüsche
werfen	warf	geworfen	würfe
wiegen	wog	gewogen	wöge
ziehen	zog	gezogen	zöge

Solutions

Lösungen zu den schriftlichen Übungen-
Solutions to the written exercises:

Lektion 1-Lesson 1

1) a) bin; b) sind; c) heißen; d) heißt; e) Kommt; f) kommen; g) Hast;
   h) habe; i) sprechen

2) a) 3; b) 1; c) 5; d) 6; e) 7; f) 2; g) 4

Lektion 2-Lesson 2

1) a) Sie; b) es; c) sie; d) du; e) wir; f) ihr; g) ich; h) du

2) a) Kinder; b) Frauen; c) Männer; d) Straßen; e) Herren; f) Radios;
   g) Menschen; h) Kinos; i) Städte; j) Länder; k) Freunde;
   k) Freundinnen; m) Kollegen; n) ——

Lektion 3-Lesson 3

1) a) Der; b) Der, dem, den; c) der; d) Der, dem; e) die; f) dem;
   g) Der/Die, dem, das; h) Der, der; i) Die, den; j) Der, dem;
   k) Das, der; l) Das, dem

2) a) Wann; b) Was; c) Was; d) Was; e) Wohin; f) Wo; g) Wo; h) Wem; i) Wohin

Lektion 4-Lesson 4

1) a) ist; b) hat; c) haben; d) bist; e) habt; f) haben; g) sind; h) hat; i) bin; j) hast

2) a) t; b) t; c) en; d) en; e) en; f) t; g) t; h) en; i) t; j) en

Lektion 6-Lesson 6

1) schloss; 2) kam; 3) wollte; 4) trafen; 5) öffnete; 6) gingen; 7) suchten;
8) könnten; 9) nahmen; 10) lernten

Lektion 7-Lesson 7

1) weil; 2) weil; 3) weil; 4) obwohl; 5) obwohl; 6) weil; 7) weil; 8) obwohl;
9) obwohl; 10) weil

Lektion 8-Lesson 8

1) Das Auto wurde an der Tankstelle gewaschen.
Das Auto ist an der Tankstelle gewaschen worden.

2) Andreas wurde von Herrn Lehmann geholfen
Andreas ist von Herrn Lehmann geholfen worden.

3) Der Zimmerschlüssel wurde den Hotelgästen gegeben.
Der Zimmerschlüssel ist den Hotelgästen gegeben worden.

4) Weimar wurde von vielen Touristen besucht.
Weimar ist von vielen Touristen besucht worden.

Lektion 9-Lesson 9

1) liefe; 2) gingen; 3) machtet, 4) käme; 5) vergäße; 6) bestelltest;
7) reservierten; 8) besuchten; 9) verlöre; 10) sähest

Lektion 10-Lesson 10

1) Die Mutter meiner Mutter ist meine Oma.

2) Die Schwester meines Vaters/meiner Mutter ist meine Tante.

3) Der Bruder meines Vaters/meiner Mutter ist mein Onkel.

4) Der Sohn meiner Schwester/meines Bruders ist mein Neffe.

5) Der Sohn meines Onkel/meiner Tante ist mein Cousin.

6) Der Mann meiner Schwester ist mein Schwager.

7) Die Mutter meiner Oma/meines Opas ist meine Urgroßmutter.
Die Oma meiner Mutter/meines Vaters ist meine Urgroßmutter.

Lektion 11-Lesson 11

1) fahre; 2) komme; 3) führen; 4) sei; 5) habet; 6) besuchen würde;
7) mitbrächten; 8) könne; 9) müsse; 10) sei

Lektion 12-Lesson 12

Beispiellösungen:

1) ..., auf dem Autos parken

2) ..., das hoch ist.

3) ..., das farbige Bilder zeigt.

4) ..., das auf Flüssen fährt.

5) ..., das Filme aufzeichnen und abspielen kann.

Notes